My Difficult And Humorous Quest
Becoming An Attorney Who Made A Difference

RES IPSA LOQUITUR

ROBERT M. MORGAN, ESQ.

ISBN: 9798847902168

TABLE OF CONTENTS

To James E. Moore, III. I could never have accomplished so many of my goals without your guidance, support, and patience. Also, thanks for not giving up on me.

To my parents for picking up the phone every time I called to complain about law school. Never would have graduated (with honors, by the way) without your help and support.

PROLOGUE

I t is so cliché to hear someone say they are pursuing a certain career or activity for "helping" others or changing the world. What does the word "help" mean anyway? Is it doing something for nothing? Or is it making a charitable contribution? In my case, is it providing free legal services and advice?

I first discovered the need to help others while in high school, volunteering for the Big Brothers/ Big Sisters program in my hometown of Richmond, Virginia. I cannot explain the absolute joy I had mentoring the young man assigned to me. He had no father in his life; his mother had two jobs and could not always be there for him. After I met and interacted with my little brother, I knew right there and then that helping others was my goal in life. The feeling is unexplainable; it is one of those things you know when you see it. In law, there is a legal theory called Res Ipsa Loquitur. This is legalize for "it speaks for itself, it is so obvious." I had drunk the Kool-Aid; it was time to discover what I needed to do to achieve this goal and still be able to make a living.

I was an under-motivated student. My grades were average. If not for the fortune of having a beautiful, extremely smart, and talented girlfriend (Donna, if I never thanked you, I just wanted you to know I would never have gone so far without you), I may have never graduated from high school. Although I have always been a hard worker, I had no idea what I wanted to do. I could work in the family furniture business or go to graduate school. But, the problem was that I did not know what graduate work I should pursue or if I could even get admitted into a graduate program after attending college.

I knew two things at the time of college graduation: First, I needed a job or to continue schooling to obtain a job to eat and have a roof over my head. Second, I wanted the opportunity to help those less fortunate than me.

This memoir contains my experiences, good and bad, in achieving this quest. Becoming a lawyer was not anything I knew about in high school and even throughout college. I did not have a Perry Mason or LA Law complex (if you are too young to know about these television shows, you really should stream them). Whenever I heard anything about lawyers, it was always in a negative light; everyone I knew hated them. I did not know any attorneys or take any pre-law, history, or political science classes in college to prepare for law school. I was just a person trying to complete a quest. After our family business was sold, the job I thought and pursued was unavailable. I researched alternative career choices; it looked like becoming a lawyer gave me the tools to accomplish my goal. I did not know, however, what a wild and crooked road it would be.

I made it and became an attorney. And after a few hiccups here and there, I found an area of law that suited not only my skill set but also furthered me on my quest.

I hope you enjoy my life journey. The bad times had me wanting to quit my quest. But, as Arnold Schwarzenegger said in one of my favorite movie lines, "If it bleeds, you can kill it!" I never thought I would be quoting Arnold; however, I always use that line whenever I try to help my children, lecture or teach law school students and others to get through tough times. It has always helped me push through the negative aspects of my life.

By the way, if you have ever visited a lawyer's office, you probably saw legal books all over the bookshelves. Trust me; your lawyer has not read every book. The books look impressive but do not be fooled by the more books a lawyer has makes them better than any other lawyer. They are for show. If you do not read past this prologue just wanted to make sure you at least got something out of reading this.

I also want to thank all my family and friends who helped me along the way. If I don't name you or I mess up on any facts, please forgive me. It was not intentional. As I have heard it said, "Never let the truth get in the way of a good story." The best place to start my quest is the beginning, so here we go.

Cheers,

PART I

MY SCHOOL YEARS

Chapter 1
THE APTITUDE TEST

While waiting in homeroom for the first period to begin, my guidance counselor called to notify me that my presence was requested in her office. I was wearing my typical green corduroy pants and a pink button-down shirt. In 1978, in my school, my clothes screamed out preppy. You were both considered preppy and a jock or you were a freak. The freaks smoked. I sometimes hung out with the freaks; in my opinion, they were more interesting than the jocks. No smoking or drugs for me; I just enjoyed the interaction and knowing not everyone was homogenous.

Walking down the hallway, I could feel the hair on the back of my neck rising. Every time the guidance counselor wanted to see someone, it was usually due to screwing up something badly or being awarded an academic scholarship. Of course, considering my grades, a scholarship was remote.

My guidance counselor was not a preppy. She was dressed very conservatively and did not have a smile on her face as I entered her office.

As usual, all the diplomas on her wall were in perfect alignment and her desk clear of clutter. Obsessive-compulsive to the max.

I figured that the purpose of my "invitation" was to discuss my result of an aptitude test all seniors took prior to graduation. My grades were average, and I was not a troublemaker. In addition to being considered preppy, I was also a jock; I was on the tennis and track teams. I mean, I could hit tennis balls against a backboard for four hours and enjoy myself. I hated reading or spending more than a half hour doing homework. My grades suffered from my lackadaisical attitude towards school.

I just liked to go by the beat of my own drum. My indifference to most things, especially with high school grades, grated on my counselor. She felt I was a typical spoiled brat who knew everything. I was mad because I knew she was right.

After exchanging pleasantries, my counselor got right down to it. She had meetings all day with students that would be a better use of her time. But, just as I thought, this meeting was to discuss my aptitude test results.

She explained that, in her experience, the aptitude test was a pretty accurate indicator of what students should do after high school graduation. In my school, the majority of my classmates were going to college, while some would go to trade schools. I knew I wanted to go to college because, growing up, my parents told me I was. I did not know there was another option.

Part of the aptitude test required a list of professions a student wanted to pursue after graduation. I put down, in order, that I wanted to be a doctor, a lawyer, or a business manager. I mean, what did I know about these professions? I thought the test wanted me to answer that way since that is what white middle-class kids should do.

Unfortunately, my test results indicated I would have better luck pursuing other careers, such as either becoming a farmer, an actor, or a professional athlete. I was a 5'11" Jewish kid from the suburbs. I knew for sure that I wouldn't be a professional athlete. Farming? I had never mowed my grass, so what did I even know about becoming a farmer? An actor sounded cool; however, I did not think my parents would send me to college to learn Shakespeare.

We had a family furniture business. My grandfather started it. I worked there every weekend and on days when they needed extra help. He always told me how he would love to have me come and work with him in order to take over the business one day. In my mind, I knew I had a backup profession waiting if I needed one. I looked up to my grandfather; he wasn't able to complete grade school since he had to work to ensure his family had food on the table. His father didn't work and died at an early age. My grandfather was a delivery driver. He would ride his motor scooter through the streets of Baltimore, Maryland, in the ice and snow. He was a hard-working man with a mission to become something more than a delivery driver. And he did it. Then, I figured it was in my DNA to do it too.

The guidance counselor advised I should consider trade school after graduation. She did not believe I was "college material." Pretty sure she also did not think quoting Shakespeare was my natural calling. Actually, I think her exact words were, "you are wasting your and your family's time and resources attending college." I was dressed like a preppy and had to go to college. I mean, I listened to what she said, and I told her I disagreed.

Later that day, after school, I discussed the test results and my counselor's advice with my parents. We discussed the results and my choice of colleges (Ok, maybe it was more yelling than discussion). My lack of motivation for school work was likely due to my having undiagnosed ADHD and anxiety. Looking back at my high school years, I could not disagree with that assessment. My parents wanted me to apply to college but wanted me to look at out-of-state schools. They said I needed to mature. They both attended out-of-state schools, which worked well for them. They thought that would be best for me, too.

That same afternoon was the typical Richmond, Virginia weather for November, with freezing rain and ice on the streets. I drove to the public library to look at college catalogs and find a school that would take me. I was among the few brave souls to venture out in this weather. I had on three layers of clothing and a winter jacket. I was freezing.

I started with the A's. I saw a catalog for Arizona State University. I could not find any specific grade requirements necessary for admission. However, I found pictures of co-eds in shorts and t-shirts. They were all huddled by a beautiful water fountain. Looking closer at the picture, I noticed it was dated in November of the prior year. Here I was in November in Richmond, wearing three layers of clothing and a winter jacket and freezing. It was serendipity; Arizona State was where I wanted to go. I would worry about what to major in later. The cost was no problem. I would take out student loans and figure out a way to pay them later. I was so excited to the extent that I ripped out the application from the catalog (you aren't supposed to do that, but I figured I was not going to "catalog jail" if caught) and sent it in that same day.

As fate would have it, I was accepted two weeks later. I was on my way to college, aptitude test and my guidance counselor's advice be damned.

Looking back to my meeting with my guidance counselor, the test results and my counselor's advice may have been somewhat more accurate than I had given it credit.

Chapter 2

MY UNDERGRADUATE YEARS

I did not know I would have to work my ass off to only get a 1.9 grade point average during my first semester in college. I was advised at freshman orientation to take 18 hours of class work and labs. That's crazy! I had 6 classes and 3 labs. I was absolutely exhausted. My failure of learning how to study had finally caught up to me. I was on academic probation, and my long-term prospects for staying in Arizona to complete my undergraduate studies looked bleak.

In high school, my smiling and beautiful girlfriend (I surely hope she is reading this) lent me her study outlines. She was brilliant, and the outlines were first-class. I achieved a B average in high school using them. If I had used them more than 10 minutes prior to each test, I probably would have been valedictorian of my class. However, now that I was in Arizona and she was in college 2,500 miles away in Virginia, I did not have anyone producing outlines to study. I was on my own. My attitude about school had to change quickly.

I was having a great time; unfortunately, I also got the grades I deserved. I lacked essential study skills. Immediate action was required if I was going to stay at Arizona State. My parents warned me that if my grades did not materially improve, I would return home to work and attend junior college. Attending junior college was probably the right thing to do at that point in my life. However, I wanted to stay in Arizona. Therefore, I made staying in college my number one priority.

Whenever I was tired or did not think I could study anymore, I thought of my little brother from the Big Brothers program. This reminded me I had a goal. I needed to "butch up" and do what was necessary to stay in school.

Upon my return to Arizona for the winter semester, I started a new routine. I went to the library every day after dinner for at least two (2) hours. I would spend my time reading assignments and studying. If I completed my work in less than 2 hours, then I pulled out magazines from the stacks and read them. To study, I made up my way of outlining. I am a visual learner. I needed to organize my notes to accommodate my learning style.

Also, I set up my course schedule to take all my classes so that I was done by noon each school day. This left me plenty of time to work out and play sports. It also allowed me to attend reverse happy hours with my friends in the evenings; this way, I was not missing out on all the things I enjoyed about college.

I also learned that you could major in just about any subject to attend graduate school, including, in my situation, law school. I assumed you had to major in pre-law, philosophy, English, or political science to attend law school. This is a very common and misunderstood fact. If you want to attend graduate school, you can major in just about any discipline. The key was looking at the graduate schools you wanted to attend and see what classes were important or required by that school for the profession you were pursuing. Not all graduate schools had the same requirements.

By the time graduation came around, I had raised my grade point average up to 3.3. I ended up majoring in Business Administration. This major allowed me to take a few business and real estate law classes. I really enjoyed those classes. The subject came naturally to me.

Chapter 3

GOOD NEWS/BAD NEWS

The dreaded phone call came late on a lazy Friday evening. I was relaxing in my fraternity house and getting ready for the weekend when I received a call from my parents.

I was a senior. I really did not know what I wanted to do regarding work. I knew I wanted a job that would allow me to make a living and still be able to help others. I am not the best business person; if possible, I want to volunteer for the rest of my life. Unfortunately, I did not have a trust fund or other assets to let me do this.

Reality told me I had to have a good-paying job so I could pay my student loans. I would just have to volunteer on my own time once I got employed. I had been pushing my decision on my long-term job prospects for as long as possible. I loved undergraduate school. I thought I could apply for a

Masters in Business Administration, which would allow me to defer deciding what I wanted to do for at least another 2 years.

The call changed all this. My father called, and we started discussing school and football. Then, he got to the reason why he called.

"Son, how are you doing?"

"Fine, dad. Just sitting around with my roommate deciding what to do this weekend."

"I have some news for you."

"What is it?"

"Well, I have good news and bad news. What do you want to hear first?"

"Let's try the good news first."

"Ok, we have decided to sell the furniture store; your mother and I are relocating to Miami and moving as soon as the sale closes."

"Ok, the bad news?"

"You are not part of the deal. You need to decide where you would like to work."

Utter silence. I was not part of the "deal?" To say I was in shock understated my feelings at this news. My fallback job was no more. I had to figure out what I wanted to do. Procrastination was no longer an option.

My thoughts about the situation were getting jumbled. I needed to speak with someone about this new development. I loved my current counselor; I called him a few minutes after my father's call.

After discussing the phone call with my father and what I wanted to do with my life, my counselor advised law school was my best option. I never thought about law school. The only thing I knew about the law was what I saw on TV.

My counselor told me about the law school admission test. I thought he was saying I needed to take the LAST; however, upon further review, I discovered he was actually saying I needed to take the LSAT, the national law school aptitude and admissions exam.

I saw the next testing date was in a couple of weeks. I did not believe I had the correct major to attend law school. My counselor advised that graduating with any major should work. This was news to me at that time. It looked like the law was going to become my career.

I discussed my long-term goal of helping people with my counselor. He advised law school should be perfect for my quest. There were many areas of law where helping others was available to me. We discussed my becoming a criminal prosecutor and putting criminals away was a way for me to go. I could also work for Southern Poverty Law Center and other free legal service providers.

I was excited after the call. I could be the guy wearing the white hat; putting away criminals was a good business since there was always plenty of crime. This could even allow me to work in any state I wished, as prosecutors are always in demand. But, I was still so naive. As discussed later, my introduction to criminal law was not very encouraging. But, at the time, I needed a fallback plan; law school sounded like the winning ticket for me!

Chapter 4

LAW SCHOOL COSTS HOW MUCH?

D eciding that I wanted to attend law school was the easy part. Now, I had to figure out how to pay for it and find a school that would take me. Unlike my research into undergraduate school, law school brochures did not have pretty pictures of the campus and students. I had to find a school that was within my budget and my ability to get student loans to attend. One thing I learned was that law schools are expensive.

Law schools take in new students annually. Most start their studies in the fall semester or quarter, depending on the school's calendar year. Law schools only require one professor to teach a course. This means that regardless of the law school you attended (i.e. Ivy League and non-Ivy League), students learn from a law professor using the same books. Law students take on approximately $30,000.00 to $40,000.00 or more yearly debt to attend and graduate.

I was also shocked to learn law schools do not typically require a student to take any trial preparation classes or go through internships, like medical schools. Instead, law school is said to be autodidactic. In other words, you are teaching yourself the law with the assistance of the professors. The purpose of the professors is to ensure students stay on track and learn areas that the American Bar Association (ABA) deems necessary. This way, all law school graduates know certain areas of the law; however, they do not learn how to practice law. Knowing the law and practicing the law were two very different things.

How would you like your surgeon to tell you, "don't worry about anything; I read a book and know how to do this procedure, trust me."

So, what are you paying for in law school? Hopefully, to have good professors who can explain the textbook's information and make it understandable so that when law students graduate, they are not committing malpractice.

Since my parents retired and sold the family business, I had to make a hard financial decision. Do I attend law school, try to get a Master in Business Administration, or go home and start looking for a job?

My father and grandfather would always tell me whatever job I pursued, make sure I could get a license in an area of business I liked so I could always be my own boss if working for others was not working out.

Based on this great advice, I chose to go the law school route. When you graduate from law school, you can take a bar exam. Upon passing the bar exam, you receive a license to practice law. You can always be the boss and have the means to make a living.

My biggest problem was that I was horrible at standardized test taking and no longer had in-state residency status to pay in-state tuition. I lost my Virginia residency when my parents moved from Virginia to Florida. Also, my parents had not been in Florida long enough for me to obtain residency through them. Since my parents considered me a tax deduction, I was never an Arizona resident. This meant I was a man without a state. Therefore, I was considered an out-of-state student wherever I applied. In addition, it implies that I was paying the highest tuition rates regardless of whether I attended a state law school or a private one.

Chapter 5

LAW SCHOOL HERE I COME

T here is an old adage I learned growing up. Whether good or bad, things come in groups of three. Unfortunately, in my situation, I lost my backup career plan due to our family business being sold and also finding out I had no in-state residency tuition rates available to me when applying to law schools. In other words, I would have to pay full freight for any law school I was interested in attending.

So, what could the trifecta be for me on what I considered a bad streak? I think I found the third item when investigating applications to law schools.

It was time. Applications for law schools that interested me were due in only a few weeks. I needed to attend a school with a history of high student bar passage rates. It is a known fact that going to school in a state where you wanted to live and practice made it easier for students to study and pass the required bar exam. Those schools offered elective courses in that state's particular laws.

The one thing going for me was I had my ace in the hole, my uncle Arvin. He was a medical school professor and ran departments at very prestigious institutions. Since I was going to be the first in my immediate family to apply to graduate school, I knew I needed his advice.

I was nervous about making the call. I was worried that uncle Arvin would think I was crazy about applying to graduate school. He knew I was not the best student. I did not know if I was going to have him laugh over the phone, or maybe he would just be so shocked he would not even be able to respond. I always thought the world of my uncle. I did not want to disappoint him or even make him feel uncomfortable if he did not think I was made of the right stuff to attend law school.

I called my uncle the next day after having found the courage.

"Robert, how're you doing?"

"Uncle Arvin, things are great! I am ready to graduate from college, and I need to discuss my options for furthering my education with you."

"What are you interested in doing?

"Well, as you are probably aware, the family furniture business was sold. So, working in the store was the first easiest option I considered. However, knowing that is no longer an option, I discussed my situation with my college counselor. Based on my long-term interests, he thinks law school is the place for me. Any thoughts?"

At this point in the conversation, I could not even remember breathing as I waited to hear his opinion.

"Law school sounds great! I know we spoke about how much you enjoyed taking law course electives. I think this is a great idea."

"I have to say I was really nervous making this call and getting your advice. I know I am no Phi Beta Kappa."

"Robert, I am on a committee where we review medical school applications. We wanted to get away from just accepting students who majored in the sciences. Heck, we recently admitted a music major who took the required science courses for medical school admission. We need students who can speak and relate to patients; we need to produce physicians with a good bedside manner; students who have a passion for not only medicine but also outside hobbies."

"Well, I really think law school may be a good fit for me based on my interests. My GPA is good enough for the schools I am looking into; I just do not have the experience of what is expected in graduate school."

"Robert, as long as you are motivated and you can say you will give law school a real chance, then shoot for the moon! Apply and see what happens. They can't repossess your education if it does not work out the way you thought. If you do not get in the fall class, you can always apply later after taking more undergraduate classes or just taking a year off from school and decompressing."

I absolutely was motivated, and I figured that if I did not like the law as a profession, I could always consider a Master in Business Administration (MBA).

My uncle's advice was to apply where I thought I could be accepted but also to consider applying to a specific school he was familiar with and with whom he knew the former dean of students. I thought he told me it was called the Mississippi School of Law. It was located in Jackson, Mississippi. The tuition was reasonable. He said he would try to contact the former dean of students and have an application forwarded to me.

His tip was to call the former dean the minute we got off our phone call; he said to drop his name and explain my situation for wanting to go to law school.

I did it!

There was another lesson I learned growing up. It was never to assume. When in doubt, double-check the source of any information that does not sound correct. Just like the saying about assumptions, "if you assume, you could end up making an ass out of you and me."

This was a lesson I kept learning throughout my entire legal career and life as I navigated my way into a profession I knew nothing about.

An application was overnighted to me. We did not have the internet back then to download an application or provide me with an option for further research into the school other than what my uncle and I discussed. I applied that same day. So what if I did not know everything about this particular law school? It was approved by the American Bar Association. This meant on graduation, I could take the bar exam anywhere I wanted to live and work. I figured the old saying about assumptions didn't apply in this situation; boy, was I surprised.

Chapter 6

WHAT WAS THE NAME OF THAT LAW SCHOOL AGAIN?

After speaking with my uncle, I felt pretty good about how I would proceed. I had a plan. There was just one thing that was nagging at me. My uncle had a very dry sense of humor. Sometimes I miss it when he is joking. An example is probably in order.

While attending Arizona State, I met students from all over the United States. One such friend is Rocco Mandala from New Jersey. Yes, I had a good friend named Rocco from New Jersey. He looked the part, but I was pretty sure he did not do any side collection work for the mafia. I like to compare Rocco to my dog, Rocky. Rocky is a pit bull/boxer mix. When our daughter brought Rocky home, I admit I was scared. He looked ferocious. But like most things, the bad is not as bad as it seems. When I got the courage to pet Rocky, he would not stop licking me and wanting to play. That's Rocco: he looked part of a cast member on the Sopranos, but he was harmless.

After completing a semester at ASU, Rocco wanted to take a road trip with me, driving home to Virginia. From there, he would fly out of Richmond and go home. We had a great time. Our route happened to take us through Mobile, Alabama, where my uncle and his family resided. I stopped there after a long day's driving.

While we were having dinner, Rocco, not known for always saying the right thing at the right time, advised my uncle he was having horrible constipation. Everyone at the table started choking on their orange chicken. Rocco knew my uncle was a doctor; I guess he figured he could get some free medical advice. My uncle advised he had the exact thing for Rocco.

After eating and watching some TV, my uncle gave Rocco some red pills. It was from a large container. Nothing on the label warned of what was to come. Rocco took a couple of these pills at my uncle's suggestion. The rest of the night was uneventful; we went to bed early as I wanted to get us to Richmond the following day.

At midnight, Rocco confided in me that his constipation was not improving. He wanted me to see if he could have some more of these special red pills he was given earlier. My uncle was only too happy to supply

Rocco with exactly what he wanted. In fact, he snickered when he gave them to him.

We pulled out of Mobile, Alabama, early the following day so we could try to make it to Richmond by dinner time. Not fifteen minutes after pulling out of Mobile, Rocco's stomach started making very loud and disturbing noises. Rocco said he was fine, and we just kept driving. Not a half hour later, Rocco saw a sign for a rest stop off the interstate. At Rocco's insistence, we pulled in so Rocco could attend to his "business."

Rocco returned to the car with the biggest shit-eating grin and said he felt the pills worked.

Not five minutes later, Rocco begged me to stop anywhere we could find a restroom. So we stopped. Rocco took a while returning to the car but said he was all good to go. That, of course, was until he needed to make another pit stop about five minutes from our last stop. This happened all day. I was starting to feel my uncle pulled a fast one on Rocco with these magic red pills he supplied.

This start and stop routine went on for the next six hours. We did not cover even half the mileage we were shooting for that day. After checking into a motel and Rocco running from my car to the room's bathroom, I decided to call my uncle and check on any possible side effects I should know about Rocco's pill-popping.

I will never forget hearing the loudest laugh in my life. My uncle definitely gave Rocco the right medicine for his constipation. The only problem is that he may have given Rocco too many of these magic pills.

Rocco and I did not get very much sleep that evening. However, Rocco woke up the next morning with the biggest smile I had ever seen on his face. He declared, "I'm cured!" I did not tell Rocco he was a science experiment.

We finally made it to Richmond the next day with the car windows wide open (I think you can figure out why), with Rocco smiling and telling me he never felt better!

My uncle and I still discuss that trip and the red pills to this day. Yes, he did pull a little prank on Rocco; however, to this day, Rocco has never forgotten the pills, reminding me never to take him back to Mobile again.

Was my Uncle playing one of his practical jokes on me regarding the law school he recommended? I found out soon enough.

Chapter 7
LAW SCHOOL 101

I received my acceptance letter to the Mississippi law school. I was excited. Although a number of other law schools accepted me, I felt a connection to the Mississippi school, especially because they took me first. I figured going to Mississippi would be an adventure. I needed to take on law school as a full-time job. I assumed there would be fewer distractions for me there.

The law school was in downtown Jackson; there was no real campus. A building housed the law school, and my apartment was directly across the street. Downtown Jackson, Mississippi was not large; nothing compared to Richmond and Phoenix. There was a McDonald's and Holiday Inn.

I went out the night before orientation, drank beers, and listened to music. I had a great time and was already meeting my law school classmates.

I was a little late to the orientation session early the next day. As I walked into the room, I saw most students wearing their best suits and dresses. On the other hand, I showed up in shorts and a tattered Arizona State T-Shirt. So much for first impressions.

I took one of the only seats left; I was sitting next to a big burly gentleman wearing a flannel shirt. I hoped I would blend in sitting next to him. The only thing missing in his wardrobe was a chainsaw or axe. Today, Dave Grohl of the band Foo Fighters would describe him as a "lumber sexual."

A professor was in front of the class. There were about 100 people in the orientation class. After some discussion about the school's rules, I started feeling something was wrong. The professor advised that no drinking, dancing, or smoking is permitted on campus. What!!! I never took any constitutional law classes but felt the rules seemed unusual and a tad strict for a state law school.

I tapped my new buddy, the lumber sexual, on the shoulder and asked if these "rules" were real or some joke. He looked at me, smiled and said,

"Hey, where do you think you are?"

"The University of Mississippi."

"Really, because this is not the University of Mississippi."

"Excuse me?"

"This is the Mississippi College School of Law. It's a private Southern Baptist school. The University of Mississippi was in Oxford about 3 hours north of here."

I could not see my facial expression but assumed it was one where I was in complete and total shock. Assuming once again bit me on the backside. There was more than one law school in Mississippi?

"Why, did you think you are at Ole Miss Law School?"

"Well, my uncle told me about this school. I mean, the Ole Miss medical school was here, as was the Capital and Supreme Court. I did not see anywhere about this being an affiliated religious school. I figured it was an extension of the University of Mississippi with this being the center of law and finance for the state."

"Well, buddy, you are here now."

At this point, my mind was racing. What the heck did I do? Had my uncle played one of his tricks or jokes on me? Since the school was located in the capital of Mississippi, how could this not be the state law school? Oy Vey! All I could think was, what was a nice Jewish boy doing here?

After the orientation, it was time to get our books and assignments for the start of school the next day. The first thing I did was find a pay phone and call the University Of Mississippi Law School. They had never heard of nor had an application for me. I was hoping this was just a bad dream. Unfortunately, this was not a mistake. I had, indeed, applied to a private Baptist-affiliated law school. My journey was getting ready to get really weird.

Oh, and I could not wait to talk to my uncle.

Chapter 8

MY INTRODUCTION TO THE SOCRATIC METHOD

After my initial shock of being at the "wrong" law school, there was no time to waste since the first day of classes was tomorrow.

The first day of class could not happen soon enough for me. I was looking at law school like I would be playing a sport. I am very competitive. I played tennis, ran track, and swam in my younger days. I hated losing. I figured I would approach law school the same way I would play any sport. Be prepared and practice. It seemed simple enough; however, that was before I was introduced to the Socratic Method of teaching.

My first class was Torts. I had no idea what a tort was, but I figured it out after reading the assigned reading that it was an introduction to personal injury law. You know, those guys that advertise on TV and billboards claiming no fees and costs unless they prevail in getting you a settlement. Remember, nothing in this world is free. If you ever need to retain a personal injury attorney, make sure you understand completely what you are getting yourself into. Also, if you and the attorney are not on the same page, ask if you can fire and retain someone else. It is very easy to get into a contract, but the real art is how you get out if you are not a satisfied customer.

At my desk, I had my coffee and was spread out with my casebook and legal pad. In undergraduate school, I typically took notes in class, read the assigned material, memorized it and took the test. However, law school was a very different arrangement, as I would soon come to learn.

The professor was setting up in front of the class. He looked harmless enough. I had heard he was funny. But unfortunately, I did not appreciate his sense of humor. He looked up from his notes, and my first law school class was underway.

He looked around, and his eyes fell on me. All students were required to complete a seating chart. In law school, the teachers are not supposed to play favorites. When you take exams, you must use your student number for identification; you cannot have your name written on any exam material.

Out of nowhere, I heard, "Mr. Morgan, please brief the first case."

"Happy to, professor. The case involved an injury that happened at a neighborhood cookout. Little Johnny was running around and being rambunctious. His parents were throwing the cookout. Little Johnny decided to play a trick on one of the guests. He pulled out a guest's chair as she was sitting down with a plate of food in her hands; she had no ability to stop from falling onto the concrete skirt around the pool. She hit the ground and was injured. She was taken to the hospital. About two months later, the guest retained an attorney to sue."

"Really, then who are the parties to this lawsuit, you know, the plaintiff and defendants?"

"The plaintiffs were the next door neighbors, and the defendants were the husband and wife throwing the party."

"Good! Mr. Morgan, now that you have proved to the entire class you can read English, why was little Johnny not made a party to the suit?"

"Well, little Johnny was just 10 years old; the neighbors could not sue him; he is too young. I looked up and found little Johnny could not be sued until he was at least 18."

"Interesting. Now, Mr. Morgan, tell me why the parents are named and why this case even required reading. I mean, it is cut and dried, is it not? The parents had a party, and someone got hurt on their property. So what makes this case important for our purposes?"

"That's a good question, professor. I was wondering that myself."

"I'm sorry, but did you answer my question with one of your own?"
"I guess I did, sir."

"Well, since you have no idea what you are talking about, let's get me another victim. Mr. Gabbert, what do you think?"

"I am guessing it has to do with whether the parents are liable for the actions of their non-adult child."

"I am getting tired of this already. Will someone please raise their hand and jump in and explain why this case is important for our purpose today?"

"Yes, Mr. Guice, what say you?

"Well, professor, since the chapter is about the tort of battery and the required intent to be responsible for an injury, I would say this case turns on whether little Johnny had the intent to cause the injury."

"Correct! Someone can actually answer a simple question. But, if little Johnny caused the injury, why are the plaintiffs suing the parents? They did not cause any injury."

"I am guessing they were sued since the damage occurred on their property; the parents would certainly have homeowner's insurance and possibly an umbrella liability policy. The parents were sued to get the insurance company involved to get a deep pocket to pay for the claimed damages."

"Yes!!"

"What did the court hold in this case, Mr. Guice?"

"The parents were liable for the actions of their child while on their property making the insurance carrier liable for paying some or all of the damages."

"Mr. Guice, you seem to be on the way to getting an A in this class."

I was stunned. Not because Mr. Guice got the right answer, but how does a ten-year-old have the requisite intent to cause the intentional tort of battery? Why didn't the neighbor just deliver the medical bill and expenses, tack on some reasonable monetary damage, take this information over to their neighbors and settle this matter amicably? Suing your neighbors certainly would make living next to each other very uncomfortable.

I was absolutely floored that we would get into the head of a 10-year-old child to see what his intent was regarding his actions. I read the case. It took me about 2 hours since the case was written in legalize, I had to use my law dictionary to look up almost every other word.

The professor kept asking questions about this case to other students; however, he never seemed to really answer any questions. Instead, he just kept asking the students questions and, after hearing the answers, asked more questions. This is how the Socratic Method of teaching in law school is done. You are supposed to anticipate questions and have answers ready.

As the class was ending, I noticed I had not taken any notes and had no idea why a lawsuit was filed.

After class, I packed up my books and went up front to ask the professor what the heck just happened. Why did the neighbors even sue for battery, which required intent? From my reading to prepare for class, I knew they could have sued for negligence or some other reason that would be easier to prove. Little Johnny was certainly not taking the witness stand to explain his intent in pulling out a chair and causing injury to his neighbors.

After I got to the professor to ask my questions, he invited me to meet him in his office to discuss the case.

I went to the professor's office and waited for him. He walked in, dropped his book and notes on his desk and looked at me.

"Mr. Morgan, do you really not understand this simple case we discussed in class?"

"I guess not, professor. I know a minor wasn't getting sued and has no money. Are you suggesting his parents were liable for his behavior?"

"Mr. Morgan, you have to be the dumbest first-year law student I have ever taught. The attorney sued the parents to get to their homeowner's and $1,000,000 umbrella liability insurance policies. The idea in personal injury cases is to sue anyone and everyone and let them figure out who is going to pay for the injuries."

"Professor, why not try to settle before filing the case in court?"

"Because, Mr. Morgan, that is not how our personal injury system works. You sue everyone that you can and let them figure it out."

"That way of thinking is why the courts are so full and unable to handle all the cases filed."

"So, Mr. Morgan, if you were the injured victim's lawyer, you would try settling their case first and then file suit later?"

"Yes."

"Do you know why personal injury lawsuits get filed before any settlement negotiations? Personal injury attorneys make between 30%-40% of the recovery against the insurance company. So, if you try to settle without having the insurance company involved, it means much less money for the attorney and the client."

"So, you are telling me that the personal injury attorney needs to look at where his fees are going to be paid before even making sure the injured client has a case?"

"You really are ignorant. If this case confused you, I hold out no hope of you passing torts. Good day. You should really think about whether you should be in law school."

Yep, I was thinking the same thing

 Chapter 9

PROFESSOR MARY LIBBY
PAYNE TO THE RESCUE

T he first two weeks of law school could not go by fast enough. Other than my Torts class, the other subjects first-year law students are required to take were interesting, and the professors were kind.

Unfortunately, my idea of wanting to be a prosecutor and put bad people in jail was not looking like a viable option for me. The first criminal law class had my professor walking in with 5 sharpened number 2 pencils in his left hand and his teaching materials in the other. He put down the teaching materials but did not move those pencils. Instead, he held them like some phallic symbol during the entire class.

In addition, the professor had gin blossoms covering his nose and cheeks. I am pretty sure he was an alcoholic. He had practiced as a prosecutor before becoming a professor. He worked his entire career in New Orleans, Louisiana. I think he may have partaken in one too many Mardi Grases. His class was simple enough; read the cases, and memorize the elements of each crime discussed.

I could not have been more bored. No real discussion ever took place in my criminal law class. The professor would talk about a case we had read, but then he would deviate into telling us about cases he prosecuted—his war stories.

At this point, I had never gotten the opportunity to meet with the former dean and professor my Uncle knew. I needed to meet her and see if I could pick up any pointers. I was getting behind in my class reading due to having to look almost every other word up in a legal dictionary to find its meaning. I really felt lost and helpless.

Professor Mary Libby Payne looked just like Dolly Parton sans guitar. Her dress, makeup, and voice were right out of a Southern Living magazine article. She was nice, humble, and smart as heck. We spoke for about an hour about me, my family, and my Uncle (who she loved, especially his sense of humor. The jury was still out on how I felt about that quality).

"Professor Payne, I have been here 2 weeks. I have read more in that time than I did in 4 years of college. I am behind in all my classes and exhausted. Law school was not like anything I imagined. I do not know if I could survive the first year, let alone the first semester."

"Robert, in just an hour we have spent together, I can see you are stressed. This is normal. The Socratic teaching method is very different; you must think and always be on your toes in all class."

"Ok, but I have one teacher who is a jerk and one who appears to be a recovering alcoholic that can never stay on topic."

"I bet I know the jerk. He is harmless. He loves picking on new students and trying to scare them. The other teacher is someone I also know well. This is a small law school; you are experiencing a normal adjustment period from undergraduate teaching. It is said that in the first year of law school, the teachers try to scare you to death. In the second year, they work you to death with all the classes and projects you must complete. But by the third year, they bore you to death since you are no longer scared of the professors or what they say they can do when you are unprepared."

"So, my experiences are to be expected?"

"Yep! I have a saying I'd like to use and think might be of help to you, 'you dance with the one you brought.' Don't change how you study or take notes. If you have questions, ask them. The professors really do want you to succeed. So do the same things you did in college; they worked well there; they will continue to do the same now."

We ended our meeting. I felt transformed by Professor Payne's manner and advice. Just hearing someone as successful as she was telling me this can be done, with the obvious southern accent, made me feel better. I went back to my apartment, rejuvenated. I was still exhausted. I still had all the work to complete. But, I felt like I just had to stick with it. I had already paid for the first semester of school. I mean, the bank could not repossess my education, could they?

Chapter 10

MY MISSISSIPPI
EXPERIENCE

I only knew about Mississippi while driving through it to Arizona. There are certain clichés about it being some backward agrarian state. One of the first things I noticed was that it was home to many very good colleges. I even learned you could farm catfish there, too. In my cloistered life, I had never eaten catfish and neither could I tell you what one looked like.

In addition to farming, Mississippi has a thriving gambling industry on the Gulf coast. Once again, I only heard about it but never seen or experienced it.

One thing I love to do when I go anywhere new is trying out local foods and drinks. Fried catfish was my first meal in Jackson. Even though my apartment had a little kitchen, I was too lazy or busy at any given time to cook. So, I ate out a lot.

Besides McDonald's, which was 2 blocks from my apartment, I would drive around to see if anything interested me. At the time, I did not realize it, but driving around and discovering new food was a great way to escape school work and decompress. One of my favorite meals was going to Morrison's Cafeteria and eating well-done liver and onions. After that, I would just sit in the cafeteria's dining room and take my time eating and reading the newspaper or anything else to switch off law school so I could keep my sanity.

I used to enjoy going to see the many college campuses. It was a very educated city. I enjoyed walking the several school grounds and treating them like parks. If I needed to get away from law school, I would walk a campus to clear my head.

My favorite campus was Millsaps College. This was a small liberal arts school. On Sundays, our law library does not open until late in the afternoon. The supposed reason for this was so students would attend church. But, being Jewish, I did not have that problem. So, I would get a bag of donuts every Sunday morning, grab an empty classroom at Millsaps College, do my homework, and study.

During my time in Jackson, there was an annual football game between Ole Miss and Mississippi State called the Egg Bowl. The week leading up to the game was great; the city was full of visitors, and all the restaurants ran specials. This is very similar to the annual Florida/ Georgia game held in Jacksonville, Florida. It was a neutral site game; the fans were passionate. On the day of the game, there were parades and other festivities.

Also, there was a reservoir. This was a lake near Jackson. The water was packed every weekend with boats, fishermen, and drinks. The only problem was that the county where the reservoir was located was "dry." Alcohol consumption was prohibited. This was a rule everyone knew but flaunted.

One weekend day, a young Mississippi College law professor and his wife decided to wander out and explore the reservoir area. They had at least a six-pack between them. As the story goes, a local sheriff saw the couple sound asleep enjoying the sun. He decided to question them. Once it was discovered the professor and his wife had been drinking beer, they were arrested.

Mississippi College is a proud Southern Baptist institution of higher learning. When news reached the school that one of its professors had been arrested for public intoxication, the preverbal crap hit the fan. The school summarily fired the professor, and no one was allowed to discuss the situation. This event bothered me. The professor was just relaxing and enjoying a day by the water. I always felt the only reason he was arrested was that the sheriff discovered he was a law professor who was likely too liberal to be hanging out with a six-pack by the water. Just my thought.

Chapter 11

LAW REVIEW AND MOOT COURT (HOW TO PICK A LAWYER)

In law school, there were two extracurricular activities that you need to take seriously. The highest honor and activity was being admitted into the Law Review. This activity is where second and third-year law school students write publishable legal articles. If you like to research and write, this group is definitely for you.

Law Review is an activity that is in addition to your classes. Usually, the top 10% of the student body are offered membership. Also, the editor of the Law Review can ask for other students they think are worthy to "write on" to the Law Review.

I was one of the lucky ones asked to write on to the Law Review. I was happy about the invite, but I really wanted to try my hand at being a member of the Moot Court Board. This activity and honor require helping first-year law students prepare and argue appellate court briefs.

In Moot Court, you learn how to write and research the law to prepare appellate briefs. Once the deadline for filing the briefs occurs, the students are given a date and time to argue their legal arguments to a board of 3 judges.

As I indicated earlier, most law schools do not require trial preparation classes. These classes are electives. However, the Moot Court competition was required. It always seemed backwards to me that law students were not required to take pretrial and trial classes but were required to argue appellate briefs. Appeals only occurred when a party lost at trial and wanted a further review of their claims by a higher court. About 95% of all lawsuits are settled or dismissed before trial; you can imagine how few go to the appellate court.

I chose to become a member of the Moot Court Board. I liked the students who served on this board. Since I chose to attend a smaller law school, I felt Moot Court took less time than being on the Law Review. I felt keeping my grades up was the best way for me to get hired upon graduation.

Also, it was a great power trip to have the first-year, neurotic law students trying to argue to you the merits of a fictional lawsuit. As a Moot Court judge, I was required to ask difficult questions and critique the appellate briefs submitted. Moot Court was not just a required class but also a competition.

One of the cases I judged had to do with free speech. It involved a student wearing an armband to school to protest a fictional war. The first-year students were all sitting up straight at their tables and nervous as hell.

After each student completed their oral arguments about why they thought their positions were correct, the judges had the opportunity to ask questions.

When my turn came to question the students, I proposed a hypothetical situation: instead of wearing an armband to school, I asked what if the student had made a poster and stood on the sidewalk outside the school to protest the war—stunned silence. The students' eyes were popping out wide. Finally, one of the students cleared his throat, stood up, straightened his suit jacket and said he had no idea and just wanted to pass this class. I almost choked on my glass of water.

I choked back laughter, too. Wow, this was certainly not going well for that student. As you can guess, that student did not win that case or the competition.

When I was a first-year law student, after I argued my moot court case, a third-year student who served as a judge had the tenacity to complain my legal arguments were lost on him due to the fact that he could not concentrate on my legal arguments as he could not take his eyes off my suit. He advised that no judge would ever take me or my legal arguments seriously if I continued dressing in that way. I was shocked at the notion in a real-world hearing that I could lose my case due to my appearance. After graduating from law school, I went to Brooks Brothers and bought the most expensive 3-piece blue power suit I could find. Gosh forbid I could lose a case for a real client because of my appearance.

The vast majority of the public has never heard of Law Review or Moot Court. If you are injured or have a legal dispute, I can tell you with absolute certainty choosing an attorney based on if he served on a Law Review or Moot Court Board can be a mistake. Just because a person may write and research well does not make them the best advocate for your legal matters. A former law partner of mine used to say that looking up and arguing the law can be done by any first-year law student; however, practicing law was the difficult part of this calling.

There is also a saying in law school about students who graduate. Those who made A's became law school professors, B students became judges and C students made all the big money. Finding the best attorney for your legal matter usually involves getting recommendations from family and friends.

In evaluating an attorney, I recommend looking for an attorney with an AV rating. This distinction is only obtained after submitting letters of recommendation from other lawyers and judges an attorney regularly appears before. Some states permit attorneys to say they are "board certified" or "experts" in specific areas of the law. That designation typically only requires the attorney to take a test.

For example, during a trial, I argued about the validity of a certain deed restriction prohibiting a homeowner from conducting a business out of his home. The homeowner's attorney was a double board certified real estate and trial attorney. He cited a case to the court that he said clearly made the restriction invalid. I had never heard of the case, notwithstanding all my trial work in this particular area of the law.

My paralegal was in the court, and I asked her to run to the court library and pull the case for me to review. I discovered the attorney misrepresented the case he cited to the court. The case he was referring to was some criminal law case about trespassing. It had nothing to do with our case. He made up the case and the argument. When it was my turn to discuss the law with the judge, I informed him of the misinterpretation of the law by the other attorney. We won the case. The other attorney was looking at paying money out of his pocket for his actions. By the way, the other attorney was not AV-rated.

Personally, I would rather pick an AV Rated attorney. The process is tougher than applying for certification, in my opinion. The fact judges are requested to opine on your legal ability means more to me than if my lawyer can take a test or run advertisements on the TV. Trust me, if you are considering an attorney, they obviously are good test takers or would not have graduated from an accredited law school.

Chapter 12

THE INTERVIEWING PROCESS

It happened right on schedule—the old saying about law school scaring and working you to death in the first two years. I was now a third-year law student who was bored to death. This gave me time to start sending out my resume. It was time to get serious and find a career path in the law.

I mailed over a hundred resumes to law firms in Florida and Arizona, the two states I thought I wanted to live and practice. Unfortunately, we did not have personal computers in the old days, so I had to type each letter of interest and lick every envelope. My tongue had the taste of glue for weeks after licking all the envelopes and stamps.

After the dust settled from all the mailings, I settled on two legal positions that truly interested me. The first was the United States Navy Judge Advocate General Corp (commonly referred to as the JAG). Unlike the television show by the same name, I did not think every day of my life would become a life and death experience practicing law. I figured the hardest part of this position would be keeping my dress white uniforms clean and learning to salute. The other position was a real estate associate position with a law firm in Jacksonville, Florida, with a very impressive list of clients and plenty of real estate work. After my positive experiences with real estate-related classes in college, I thought this might be a good area for me to start practicing law.

The Navy offered me a four-year initial posting representing sailors accused of crimes. I would have to learn about Captain's Masts and Mutiny laws and procedures; these are not offered as elective courses in most law schools.

Although I was not interested in practicing criminal law after my experience in my first-year criminal law class, the Navy offered the opportunity to defer payment on my student loans. I figured I needed a job and experience. I could get this by serving my required four-year stint. If the Navy felt I was doing a good job, they could sign me up for more tours of duty. If that did not happen, I knew I would have great trial experience; this is the one thing all legal employers want in new hires. They wanted new hires to know where the courthouse was located.

After completing all my initial interviews and testing, the last step to being offered a position with the JAG Corp was a mental and physical exam. I could only hope my sanity was still in good shape after 2 1/2 years of law school.

The weirdest part of the Navy testing process was the physical exam portion. We lucky ones looking for a commission in the Navy had to undress down to only wearing our underwear. We then were told to walk like a duck across a large room. Yes, the Duck Test.

The officer assigned to our group told us to get on our knees; this was uncomfortable due to the linoleum flooring. We were then instructed to walk like a duck, using our knees instead of our legs. We had to "walk" this way across the room. I advise anyone thinking about military duty to bring knee pads to the physical testing site. You will thank me later.

After crossing the room, we had to roll up to a standing position. This does not sound too difficult, except all our knees were bruised by the duck walking exercise. I made it; about 10 other guys did not and were escorted out of the room. Then, after putting back on our clothing, it was time for a chest X-ray and consultation with the doctor.

When I walked into the doctor's office, I was hit with the horrible smell of cigarettes; I do not mean just some smoke; I am talking about a room so full of hazy purple smoke, not even Jimi Hendrix could have sung about it. I could nearly breathe.

So, while covering my mouth and nose, I noticed the books on the doctor's bookshelves were full of treatises on pulmonary and lung disease. This was the absolute definition of irony.

After my examination, the doctor, coughing in his hand, said I was in good shape, except for some small spots on my lungs. He ordered another round of chest X-rays. This meant going back into his office and the purple haze of smoke.

When the doctor put the second set of X-rays up on the lighting element to review it, I said the spots looked similar to thumbprints. About 5 minutes later, the doctor came to the same conclusion. Both sets of X-rays were taken by the same technician[1][2]; this guy apparently left his thumbprints on everything he X-rayed. I hate denigrating anyone, but this doctor was a real quack (no pun intended).

I was given a good fitness report. I ran out of the office as fast as possible, hoping I did not actually get spots on my lung from sitting in the doctor's office.

After all the testing was completed, I returned to the Navy recruiter. He advised I was moving along nicely through the process and should know something in a week.

Learning to wear white dress uniforms and not getting them dirty when I ate looked like my future.

Chapter 13

THE REAL ESTATE POSITION

While awaiting word from the Navy, I received a phone call from a law firm in Jacksonville, Florida. I had to look up the firm to remember who they were (I had sent so many letters and resumes out that I could not tell you their names).

This was a "blue blood" law firm. That designation is typically given to medium to large-sized law firms whose clients were mostly large corporations, banks and real estate developers, and, of course, the wealthy, typically whose wealth came from old money.

When I spoke to the recruiting partner, he advised that they would love to interview me if I wanted to come to Jacksonville on my own dime. I almost forgot that blue blood firms at that time were known for being very stingy on paying for anything that could not be charged to a client.

I took the gamble. I learned that going from Jackson, Mississippi to Jacksonville, Florida was $600. No discount airlines back then. I sucked it up and went.

The interview was, in my opinion, a dud. The flight was delayed, and we did not meet until late in the day, which left me little time to speak to all those attorneys. I left with zero expectations of getting an offer from this firm. My fingers were crossed the Navy came through.

A few days later, the hiring partner called me and asked if I could be in Jacksonville to discuss the position the next day. I was floored. Forget the cost and time; we were in finals week when they called me, and my hardest subject that semester was the last test I was studying for. I did not want to go back without some assurance of a job offer. All the partner told me was I would not be disappointed.

Being young, stupid and very naive, I told the partner I did not think I would be a good fit considering how poorly my first interview went.

The partner said nothing for what seemed like an hour but was more like 30 seconds. Finally, he told me to get my butt on a plane and attend the interview. As a show of good faith, the firm bought my airline ticket, and it was waiting for me at the airline ticket counter. As you can tell, this was way before the TSA and security were added to airports.

After arriving at the interview, the first person I spoke to was the head of the litigation department. I, of course, was dressed in my three-piece Brooks Brothers suit.

"Robert, if I asked you to come into the office on the weekend because we were short-handed and we need copying done, would that trouble you?"

"Trouble me; you must be kidding. We had a family furniture store growing up. I cleaned out the warehouse, drove the delivery truck, delivered furniture, and had to clean myself off to sell if any of the salespeople failed to show up on any given day. So if you have coffee and the air conditioning was turned on, heck yes! I would do that. I'll even do a headstand if you wanted me to."

The real estate partner was next. He wanted to know how I would dress if I was invited to attend a firm marketing or client dinner.

"John, I would wear the suit I had on since it was my only one; however, if required, I would buy a new one and Khakis. I never miss out on free food!"

Lastly, one of the bank attorneys came in to interview me. He asked, "If we gave you a new file to open and you did not know what to do, how would you handle getting the required information?"

"Ed, I would come to your office and ask you; however, if you were unavailable, I would pitch a tent next to your office until I got my questions answered." He laughed, shook my hand and left the room. After meeting with a few other attorneys, I was directed to the hiring attorney's office.

The hiring partner entered the room. He said the firm would like to offer me a position as a real estate attorney. I had to hold the bottom of my chair so I would not jump up and scream.

"I would love to work here and with all of you."

"Good, then here is our offer, we will pay you $16,000 per year. You would, however, have to start immediately after graduation. Since you need to pass the Florida Bar exam, you would also be expected to study for the bar exam and work here full time. Studying would have to be on your own time."

Now, this partner did not know that one of my law school professors was a good friend and a classmate of one of the named partners in this firm. When I told the professor I was going for the second interview, he warned me that they would try to lowball on salary and figure I would take it since

I was coming from a small law school. The professor gave me an idea of how to handle this situation.

In 1985, when I graduated from law school, a manager at a McDonald's restaurant made more than $16,000 a year. I know because I asked. So, upon hearing the offer, I was ready.

"Bill, I can't thank you enough for the offer. Now, I've never lived in Jacksonville, Florida. But, if you believe that paying me $16,000 a year as my starting salary would help me bring new clients to the firm and put me in a position to meet and market to these people, then I would be happy to accept the offer."

Bill's face turned red. He excused himself and went into another office. I heard screaming and something about "how could you lowball him like that?"

Bill returned to the room. He said he would like to amend the offer.

"Robert, we will pay you a salary of $24,000 a year and pay for your parking."

Once again, I found myself holding the bottom of my seat, trying not to jump up and yell in excitement.

"Bill, let me ask you a question. First, you offered me $16,000 a year with no parking, and now, you immediately offered me $24,000 with parking. If I answer you the same way I did when you made the first offer, would I get another $8,000 raise in my salary?"

"Robert, take the offer, and, no, I am not going to give you another "raise.""

"Bill, let me think about this, and I will get back to you tomorrow. Great seeing you again, but I have to run to catch a plane and take my last final tomorrow."

Of course, I took the real estate associate position over the Navy's offer. Even if I did not get to defer my student loans, what if I figured I did not like the Navy after 4 years? This real estate position was what I thought I wanted. I'd be a fool not to take it and hope maybe a similar position would be available to me in 4 years.

I never thought getting a job would be so gut-wrenching. Jacksonville, Florida, here I come!

PART II

MY WAR STORIES

(How I Learned To Practice Law)

Chapter 14

MY FISH STORY

The first and most important lesson students and new lawyers must adhere to is never to assume. Significant legal fees are paid arguing in court over what a client or their lawyer assumes is true. An example of when you need to be careful assuming is my fish story.

I was invited to watch a football game and have dinner at a lawyer friend's home. One of my coworkers owned the home, and her husband was a local state judge.

We all had a few beers while watching the game. No one was drunk; we were just telling stories about work and current events. The judge told us he had a great story about a case he had handled.

The judge was an adamant fisherman who sometimes brought his fishing pole to court. If the weather was good and his docket light, he would sometimes sneak out in the afternoon and fish. His favorite fish to catch were snook. Since I absolutely had no interest in fishing or what a snook fish looked like, I figured the story would be boring. But was I wrong?

The case involved the alleged violation of the local fishing and hunting laws. On the stand was a Game and Fishing Police Officer. The defendant, a local sub-contractor between jobs, was sitting at the defense table in his jail outfit as he could not make bail and go home to change. The police officer was being questioned by a prosecutor who appeared to be a newly minted attorney handling his first case.

The officer was asked the typical questions about his job duties, where he was on the day the defendant was fishing, and how he handled the violation once he arrived at the crime scene.

"Officer Smith, how long have you been a Game and Fishing Officer?"

"Five years, sir."

"So, have you ever handled a case where the fishing laws have been broken?"

"Yes, sir."

"Can you please describe what happened in this case?

"Of course. I received a call to check out a subject fishing from the Sanibel Beach Bridge. When I arrived, I saw the subject. He was fishing with three fishing poles and had a cooler with him."

"Officer, was there any sign the subject was drinking?"

"No, sir. He introduced himself, and I asked for his driver's license to confirm his identity. I also asked to see his fishing license."

"Then what happened?"

"I asked what he had in the cooler. The subject said he had five fish, actually snook fish, to be precise."

"What happened then?"

"I asked the subject to open the cooler so I could see what he had caught."

"Did the defendant comply with this request?"

"Yes, sir. I looked in the cooler and saw water, where he had five fish swimming around that appeared to be snook."

"Officer, are there any special rules about snook fishing compared to any other fishing?" "Yes, local rules prohibited the capture of any snook fish under two feet."

"What did you do then?"

"I took out our special snook ruler to check the length of the fish. To my eye, they did not appear to meet the rules."

"Then what did you do?"

"I asked the subject to hold up each fish, so I could determine their length. All five snook were under the size requirements."

"Then what happened?"

"I had the subject put the five fish in the cooler I carried in my vehicle. I then arrested the subject, read him his Miranda rights and handcuffed him. After placing the subject in my vehicle, I transported him to the sheriff's office so he could be held until he could appear before a judge."

"Did the defendant admit to you anything about his actions?"

"Yes, he did. During the trip to the Sheriff's office, the subject advised he'd been fishing snook for his whole life and was keenly aware of the length restrictions to this particular sport fish."

"Did the defendant say anything else?"

"Yes. He said his father taught him from a young age how to measure snook if you did not have any special measuring equipment."

At this point, the judge interrupted the proceeding and said he had a couple of questions for the officer.

"Officer, after discovering all the fish were not the authorized length, what did you do with the fish?"

"Well, as I said earlier, I placed all five snook in my cooler and transported the fish along with the subject to the Sheriff's office."

"I am just curious, but did you ask to see the defendant's "tool" he used to determine their length?"

"Yes, I did, your honor. The subject took his shoes off and lined them up vertically so that the toe of one shoe touched the rear of his other shoe."

"Officer, did you have water in the cooler you transported the fish in?"

"No, your honor. I had dry ice in my cooler."

"Wait a minute! You're saying you arrested the defendant over a snook fishing violation, the law obviously being for the protection and sport of this fish. Then, after arresting the defendant and reading him his rights and transporting him to jail, you put five live snooks in a cooler with dry ice?"

"Yes, your honor."

"When you arrived at the jail, what did you do with the fish?"

"When we arrived at the jail, I saw the fish were dead and stored them in the cooler in the Sheriff's freezer."

"So, you killed five snook fish after arresting the defendant who actually had them in water and alive?"

"Yes, sir.

The judge turned to the defendant's public defender. "Mr. Jones, do you mind if I ask your client a few questions?"

"No, your honor."

"Sir, you admit catching the snook, correct?"

"Yes."

"Did you happen to bring with you today this 'tool' you claimed to have used to measure the length of the fish?"

"No, your honor, I did not bring the exact shoes, but the ones I am wearing are the same size."

"What do you mean you don't have the same shoes? How did you measure the snook?"

"Like I always do, I took off my shoes and laid the fish next to them to see if fish each reached the 2 Feets requirement."

"2 Feets? What is that?"

"Your honor that has always been the rule since I was a kid fishing snook. The snook had to be at least 2 Feets or you had to throw them back."

The judge, his face turning crimson, turned to the officer still sitting on the stand and asked him, "Did the defendant tell you how he measured the fish?"

"Yes, your honor."

"So, just to make sure I understand, officer, you arrested a man who was trying to comply with the game and fishing laws. You then killed the fish by putting them in your cooler, which had dry ice in it and caused the death of the fish you were protecting?"

"I guess if you put it that way, then, yes, that is what happened."

"I am trying to decide if I want the officer or both the officer and the prosecutor put in jail for plain stupidity and failure to do their respective jobs!"

The judge continued, "While I ponder how I will proceed, the court is embarrassed, to say the least. Sir, you are free to leave. I find you not guilty of any crime. You did not have the requisite criminal intent to break the law to which you were arrested. Please accept my apologies. But, please, sir, purchase a proper measuring tool at any sporting goods store in the area, so this may never happen again."

"Thank you, your honor!"

"Now on to you two!"

Everyone at the table was laughing so loud I never heard what the judge did to the officer and prosecutor. I assume they never wanted another case in front of that judge.

Chapter 15

MY FIRST LITIGATION LESSON

In November of 1985, I was handed my first litigation case. This case had been hanging around our office for over a year. The case was being handled by a partner who had left the firm; he neglected to tell anyone about this case. It just sat on his desk, gaining dust for 6 months.

The trial was fast approaching. The client had not called in all that time. When she finally did call, the litigation partners went into malpractice mode; they had to prepare for the trial which was only a few weeks away. They did not conduct all the necessary fact gathering as they had no time. What should they do? How about giving the file to the new guy?

Since I was the low man on the totem pole (i.e. my hourly rate was less than anyone else in the litigation department), the file was dropped on my desk. I told the attorneys delivering the file that I was a real estate attorney. They laughed and walked out of my office.

The case involved the failure of a party to pay a loan. We represented the plaintiff. The defendant signed a promissory note evidencing the loan. Seemed straightforward. I reviewed the file. I only had a copy of the note in the file; I could not find the original.

I did not know where the original note was located. Our client did not know, either. I contacted the opposing counsel to inquire about the original note. He advised he had not seen it. The only copy he had was the one attached to the complaint we filed against his client. The case should have been a slam dunk. To all you aspiring lawyers, there is no such thing.

On the day of the trial, I asked the defendant's attorney if he intended to call his client as a witness. He said he did not and that he had no defense to our claim. My nerve endings were starting to tingle. Something in my gut said this was not right.

It was agreed since this was a straightforward case no jury was necessary; we would let the judge hear the evidence and let him decide the outcome.

I called our client to the stand. After getting our client's name, address and other basic information, I started asking about the loan.

"Ms. Moore, can you tell us the circumstances surrounding the loan you made to the defendant?"

"Sure. Mr. Hubbard asked me for a loan of $100,000. He said he needed it for starting a new business venture. So we went to my attorney at that time. He drew up a promissory note to evidence the loan."

"Did you give the defendant the money?"

"Yes."

"Did the defendant ever make any payments under the terms of the loan?"

"No."

"Did you try to contact him about his failure to pay?"

"Yes. My former lawyer tried multiple times to get the loan paid or even to amend it to make it easier for the defendant to pay it."

"Did anything ever happen with these attempts?"

"No. He never replied to any of our overtures."

At this point, the defendant's attorney had not objected to any questions. It is typical for a lawyer to object in order to throw off the other attorney's momentum and get him confused. I knew the defendant's attorney; he was a very good and experienced trial lawyer. Nevertheless, something just did not feel right. I just could not put a handle on what it was.

"Ok, I am going to approach and show you a copy of the promissory note. Your honor, may I approach the witness?"

"Yes."

"Is this a true and correct copy of the note your former lawyer prepared and was signed by the defendant in front of you and your lawyer?"

"Yes."

"Your honor, since we are unable to find the original note, we ask this copy be admitted into evidence."

Before the judge could reply, the defendant's attorney stood and asked if he could ask our client some questions to further identify this copy of the note. The judge agreed. I sat down and the defendant's attorney pulled out a piece of paper and approached our client.

"Ms. Moore, do you recognize this document I am handing to you?"

"Yes. This appears to be the original note."

"Objection! Your honor may we approach?"

"Yes, please."

We both approached the judge. I explained that I asked the defendant's counsel if he had possession of the original note and was told he did not. This was a classic he said, she said situation. We had the burden of proof and had to prove the note had not been paid. Without the note in evidence, we had no case. The defendant's attorney argued that he had not seen the note until last night when his client advised he found it. The original and copy looked identical.

After hearing all our legal arguments, the judge said he would not allow my copy of the note into evidence but would consider admitting the original note if a proper foundation was established. In other words, that the note was, in fact, the contract between the plaintiff and defendant.

The defendant's attorney asked our client if the note he was showing her was, in fact, the original note signed by the defendant.

"Yes, it does appear to be the original note."

I did not object to any of the questions establishing the existence of the note; I mean, it helped my case. So, why was the defendant's attorney helping me?

The defendant's attorney then turned to our client on the stand and said he had one more question. "Do you see any stamps on the note?"

"Stamps? You mean like postage stamps?"

"No. I mean documentary tax stamps?"

"I don't know what that is."

I objected at this point for no other reason but to give me time to figure out what the heck was happening to this slam dunk case my partners gave me. My objections were all properly denied by the judge.

"I ask again, Ms. Moore, do you see any documentary tax stamps anywhere on the front or back of the note?"

"I don't believe so, no."

The defendant's attorney turned to the judge and objected to the original note being placed into evidence or in any way to be used as proof of the loan. His reason was by law if the note failed to have documentary tax stamps affixed to it, then it could not be admitted into evidence. He then cited a state law purporting to prove his position.

I looked at the copy of my note in my file. It was then I noticed I only had a copy of the front of the note. I assumed the plaintiff's former lawyer did whatever was necessary to make the note enforceable. Like putting the stamps on the back of the original note as was customary.

The judge said he was taking a 15-minute recess to read the law presented and to examine the original note. During this recess, my client was livid. She said I was an idiot.

I walked over to the defendant's attorney and asked why he failed to deliver the note once he knew his client had it and about the law he was using to keep the note out of evidence. The defendant's attorney was married to a tax lawyer. While he was preparing for the trial last evening, his wife told him about the law he was now using regarding the requirement of having tax stamps on the note to enforce payment. He told me in his over 20 years of litigation experience, he had never heard of the law until his wife told him about it.

The judge returned and called the court to order. He looked at me and said he had been a judge for over 30 years and had never heard about this law. I asked for another 15-minute recess so I could run downstairs to the clerk of the court's office to purchase the stamps; the law did not say when the stamps had to be purchased, just that they had to be there at the time of it being admitted into evidence.

The judge said he felt bad for me but had another trial that afternoon and had no time to give me. At this point, I was sure my client was going to strangle me; heck, I was going to strangle the partner who gave me this file (assuming my client didn't kill me first).

The moral of this story is quite simple. DO NOT ASSUME. In this case, I assumed the other litigation partners knew what they were doing, and all the information I needed was in our file. I also assumed our client's previous lawyer knew what he was doing and took all steps to make the note enforceable. I was wrong on both accounts. Our client paid for my rookie mistake. We settled the case that afternoon but for less than what we claimed.

If you are told a matter is a "slam dunk," watch out!

Chapter 16

HOW TO FIX A TICKET

W hile working with my blue blood law firm in Jacksonville, one of the partners approached me. He wanted me to take on a little favor. Of course, as there is nothing none as a "little" favor, I just smiled and said fire away.

The partner's father was ticketed for reckless driving. He was 68 and still had his driver's license with only a restriction that he wear corrective eyewear when operating any motor vehicle. The ticket could be paid or contested. The cost to make this go away was $150.00; however, the downside to this approach is it added points to the father's license. His insurance could be hiked or suspended if he paid the ticket. If he lost his insurance, he could not legally drive.

I looked into the partner's eyes and, as direct as I could be asked, "Has your father ever had a ticket or any other moving violation matter?" "Absolutely not, I mean, maybe a fender bender now and then, but nothing serious."

At this point, looking back on this conversation, I wished I had asked what "serious" meant.

The ticket had to be paid that day, or he could contest it in court in two weeks. I asked the partner, "Does your father have any points on his license? If so, taking this to trial and losing could cause his loss of driving privileges."

The partner looked me in my hazel eyes and said, "My father has no points; however, with his age, the family is worried if he were not allowed to drive he would lose his independence." What I figured was that no family member wanted the responsibility of taking care of and driving his father around.

Under the circumstances, it was decided to go to trial. Typically, the citing police officer was busy when traffic court met; that was good because the officer would not show. Without the officer present, the state's burden could not be meant as the ticket was considered hearsay and inadmissible without a proper foundation. In English, no show, we go home, and the case is dismissed.

I always liked being punctual wherever I went. Traffic court was no exception. I wore my power blue Brooks Brothers three-piece suit with a preppy blue and red tie. Noticing what the other attorneys were wearing, I looked like I was dressed to go to prom but without a date.

All the attorneys were called to see the court clerk in order to get the time of the cases being tried that day. When I reached the front of the line, the clerk said I looked new and did I have any questions. My first response was to scream, "What the hell am I doing here, and will I end up in jail if I screw up this case?"

The clerk, in a very calm and reassuring voice, said, "Since you are new and the only one of the attorneys looking like they care being here, tell the Judge when he calls your case that your client pleads nolo, requests the court to waive court mandated driving class and withhold any points on my client's license and he will pay the court costs."

I felt like I was in a movie, memorizing lines for my part. At this point, I wished Mathew McConaughey walked through the door like in his movie —The Lincoln Lawyer.

After introducing myself to the client, I explained my strategy. He did not object and just wished this whole thing was over with. Little did he know, so did I. To ensure I did not make any unnecessary mistake, I asked to see the paperwork the court sent him. I noticed his paperwork included there was an alcoholic beverage odor in his car. However, in my paperwork, my partner gave me no bottle or alcoholic beverage was noted as being in the vehicle.

One thing I learned from great attorneys, like the aforementioned Mathew McConaughey, was never ask your client if they are guilty. Instead, just present the facts truthfully and let it rip.

After finding seats, my client and I sat in the gallery and watched the cases going ahead of us. All these cases seemed to go without much drama. I noticed all the attorneys requested the same disposition of their cases as the clerk advised me. I was starting to feel more comfortable.

A distinguished but clearly underdressed attorney approached the podium next when his case was called.

"Good day, your honor. I am here representing Mike Whitefield. He was apparently ticketed for driving 45 miles per hour in a 30 mile per hour zone. At this time, we wish to plead nolo, the court waive mandated traffic school and withhold the points on his license. We will, of course, pay the court costs for this hearing."

The judge replied," Mr. Smith, is your client with you today so that I may ask him some questions?"

"Why no, your honor, my client just graduated from the University of Florida law school and is driving to Tampa to take the bar exam."

"Really, Mr. Smith. By chance, did you ask your client if he had any prior traffic violations?"

"No, your honor, I did not."

"Then good for you, as I would have you held in contempt of court."

The judge then lets sheets of computer paper fall to the courtroom floor.

"Mr. Smith, this is a computer printout of your client's traffic violations for the past three years. I can only imagine what a further review of his record would demonstrate."

"Your honor, I am appalled and will check into this with my client upon his return to Jacksonville."

"Yeah, you may want to do that. You can figure he will not have any other appointments for the next few months. Sheriff, I am issuing a bench warrant for Mr. Whitefield forthwith. I want this executed without delay. We will reschedule this matter for two months from now. How in the world did your client get permission to even sit for the bar exam? I will be contacting the Bar about this situation today.

The attorney walked back through the gallery. I'm thinking I would really hate to have to follow that guy. The next case was called. Guess who was next?

"Mr. Morgan, I see you represent the defendant in this matter; is he related to a local attorney with the same last name?"

"Why, yes, he is, your honor. I work with his son."

"That's what I thought. That's why you are here and not him, I bet."

"Your honor, is there a problem?"

"Well, your client has had a few recent run-ins with the law. This is his 4th accident within the past 3 years. Are you aware of this fact?"

"Absolutely not. In reading what the court sent to my client, none of these accidents was indicated."

"Is your client with you today?"

"Yes, your honor. Mr. Horowitz, please join me at the podium."

"Mr. Horowitz, how old are you?"

"68 years young, sir"

"Well, if you want to continue living like the rest of the citizens of Jacksonville, I should revoke your license."

I put my hands out to stop Mr. Horowitz from saying something he may regret during his remaining young years.

"Your honor, may I suggest an appropriate remedy?"

"Go ahead, Mr. Morgan."

"May we plead nolo on this charge, require driving school and that Mr. Horowitz takes another driver's exam after completing his driving course. Then, assuming he passes all of these tests with flying colors, he is permitted a license with any limitations or restrictions this court deems appropriate. Of course, he will also pay all court costs and fines."

"Mr. Morgan that is an excellent way to proceed. With these conditions being satisfied by your client in the next 90 days, we will continue this matter at a later date."

A few days later, Mr. Horowitz appeared at my office with his son, my partner. Mr. Horowitz could not thank me enough for helping him get out of this ticket in the manner we did. I bet Mr. Horowitz's children were pretty impressed by my skills, too.

Mr. Horowitz presented me with a blue velvet bag. I looked inside and saw a bottle of Chivas Regal. He said it was his favorite and not to drink and drive.

I was thankful the judge was as forgiving as he was. I never opened the bottle; I held on to it all these years later to remember being prepared is very important for any attorney, but knowing how to BS on your feet is even better.

Chapter 17

THE EXPLODING TOILET
IN PALATKA CASE

I truly intended to be a real estate attorney; that was why the firm hired me. However, the firm's litigation department was slammed with work. They needed help, cheap help. That's me.

In December 1985, the next litigation case they handed me seemed straightforward. A client developed low-income rental housing. One of the many client's tenants had a plumbing complaint. She hired an attorney to sue our client for damages arising from her toilet exploding. I had to read the file twice to make sure I was reading it correctly. I was having trouble visualizing this. As horrible as this sounded, I could not stop laughing. I mean, law school did not prepare me for this crap (pun intended).

I set up the plaintiff's deposition. A deposition is when you take the testimony of a party or witness to a lawsuit. It is a way to lock a person into their story and what they would testify to at trial. If she described this incident differently than during her deposition, her credibility could be attacked. I also requested copies of all documents she possessed demonstrating the damages she alleged occurred due to her...hmmm, toilet exploding.

If the facts described in the lawsuit were true, I really felt bad for the tenant. I did not want her getting less than she was entitled to if my client was liable for the explosion. I just could not figure out how she survived her toilet exploding as she described in her lawsuit.

With our client's permission, I hired a private investigator and plumbing expert to assist in my preparation for the trial. Plaintiff swore she was not settling; she wanted a trial.

Our plumbing expert provided me with a report indicating there was no way her toilet exploded as she described. He believed that she would have gone head first through her bathroom ceiling and would likely not live to tell the tale. He figured someone put firecrackers in the toilet.

In my three-piece suit, I appeared at the courthouse in Palatka, Florida, where the case was filed. The plaintiff and her attorney were both present. They appeared to be excited at the prospect of getting a huge settlement or verdict if this case went to trial. I absolutely did not want this matter going to trial. I mean, I would not be able to stop laughing long enough to present this case to a jury in Palatka.

I started with the easy stuff first. "Ms. Smith, could you tell the court reporter your full name and address?"

"My full name is Sally Smith. I live in Palatka, Florida."

"Do you still reside in the apartment owned by our client where the alleged injury occurred?"

The plaintiff's attorney jumped in, "There is no alleged injury; the toilet exploded with her on it!"

"Ok, Mr. Jones, would you like me to swear you in to be a witness, and I can take your deposition while I'm in town today?"

"You're skating on thin ice, Mr. Morgan. You are not from around these parts. Be careful."

"Wait a minute, are you threatening me about your allegation that your client survived a literal spaceship launching in her bathroom? I know we are near Cape Canaveral, but threats really are not necessary."

I knew her attorney would try to be aggressive. He wanted to show who was the boss to his client. The partners in our litigation group warned me this might happen; I was ready for it. I was locked and loaded. The private investigator's report and the on-site manager's information were helpful to our defense.

"So, Ms. Smith, can you please describe what happened on the day both before and after your toilet malfunctioned?"

"Malfunctioned? The toilet exploded!"

"Let's not get caught up in semantics, and please continue." Her attorney told her to continue.

"I woke up early and drove to Daytona Beach to get some sun and relax. Upon returning home to my apartment, I needed to use the restroom. While doing my business, the toilet exploded and shot me head first into the ceiling. Water gushed everywhere, destroying all my cherished personal possessions."

Her attorney was giving me his best stare down

"I see. When did you start drinking on that day?"

"Objection!"

Ms. Smith looked surprised by my question. She turned to her attorney for advice. Her attorney responded, "Answer the question."

"Well, I do not remember saying I was drinking, but, yes, I guess I did drink a few beers that morning."

"What time did you start drinking?"

In preparing for this deposition, I checked the Palatka public records and found that the plaintiff had a history of DUI citations. Also, the property manager told us the plaintiff was never outside her apartment without a can of beer in her hands. So I asked the question to rattle her. Experience always pays; I was not asking her any questions to which I did not know the answer.

"Well, I would say around 8 AM that day."

"What time do you typically start drinking alcoholic beverages?"

"Objection!" roared her attorney. "Do not answer that question. Mr. Morgan, I intend to report you to the Florida Bar for your unprofessional manner."

"I am still waiting for an answer to my question. If you advise her not to answer, I will have the court reporter certify the question and have her answer them in front of the judge. Of course, you will have to pay my attorney fees in that event."

"Ok, Ms. Smith, let me ask another question. Could you remove your hat, please?"

"What! Why do you want me to take my hat off my head?"

"You alleged you were thrown into your bathroom ceiling about 4 weeks ago. It has not been that long since the incident. I just want to see what injuries you suffered and ensure you receive any necessary medical treatment. Scaring, bumps, and abrasions, are the types of injuries one is likely to sustain. I mean, you have those injuries, don't you?" Based on the pictures the manager sent us, I knew she did not suffer any head trauma.

Three things are important at this point. First, our on-site property manager indicated the plaintiff walked around constantly without any bandages or hats since the date of the "accident."

Second, during a deposition, you are permitted to ask any questions that are reasonably directed at finding relevant evidence. Again, courts take a very liberal view of this rule. This means almost any question you want to ask is valid as long as it relates to the case and can be used to get to the truth of the matter.

For example, when working for a large interstate law firm, one of the litigation partners told a story about how he re-plumbed his master bathroom. He was taking the deposition of a contractor. The partner decided to ask questions about plumbing that were totally unrelated to the case. However, the partner advised all the parties he was trying to ensure the contractor was a credible expert witness. That attorney ended up asking questions about the remodeling of his master bathroom. The attorney literally had the contractor answer all the questions the partner had so he could do the remodeling himself. You've got to love the law!

Lastly, if a witness fails to answer a question asked of them, and the judge finds that the question is permissible (which they almost always do), the losing party typically pays the attorney fees of the prevailing attorney. That is an expensive bet directing a client not to answer any questions and hope you will prevail at a hearing on the matter, especially in light of the broad definition of what is permitted to be asked.

Directing the court reporter to "certify" the question was something I learned the night before reading a book on how to take effective depositions. That book will now have a permanent place next to my bible (well, not being Catholic, I think you know what I mean).

Ms. Smith's attorney started to sweat. Finally, her attorney asked if we could adjourn for 10 minutes. This is what I was hoping would happen. I know the attorney prepared his client for the deposition, but I was sure he did not think I would find her DUI citations and her being probably an alcoholic based on the on-site manager's comments.

"Ok, let's take a 10-minute break."

After about 5 minutes, the plaintiff's attorney asked if we could discuss an issue regarding the case in private.

"Sure, happy to talk." We walked out into the corridor.

"Mr. Morgan, is your client willing to settle this case for $100,000.00?"

"I know for a fact that amount is out of the question. I discussed settlement authority with my client prior to taking this deposition. My settlement authority does not exceed $25,000.00. This amount is what we figured it would cost my client in attorney fees to defend this lawsuit. This is the best offer you will get."

I continued, "I am looking forward to hearing how your client explains how her toilet exploded, and she is still alive to tell the tale."

"We'll take the $25,000.00 as long as it is delivered or wired to my office by tomorrow."

"No worries. I'll just need your firm's trust account information to wire the money, and a signed agreement to have this litigation dismissed with prejudice. Our client will not admit any fault and we require mutual releases of liability so that we won't be bothered with this issue again."

I really did not think we could win this case in a trial before a jury in Palatka, Florida. But, with the DUI information and common sense about her being launched from her toilet into the ceiling and being able to tell the tale, I convinced my client to give me some settlement authority so we could end this matter.

This litigation stuff is fun. But I still thought I wanted to be a real estate attorney. I thought being a real estate attorney would give me the personal time I needed to volunteer at Big Brothers/Big Sisters and other worthwhile organizations. Litigation requires hours of discovery, legal research, and traveling. It is very stressful unless your brain is wired to handle the stress and anxiety. I wasn't sure my brain was, but I enjoyed litigation. What did I know?

On the 2-hour ride back home, I loosened my tie and opened the windows singing along to a Lynyrd Skynyrd tape as loud as I could.

Fun fact, Lynyrd Skynyrd was from Jacksonville. So it just felt right to sing and listen to them all the way home.

Chapter 18

WHEN DOES A ROSE SMELL LIKE MANURE

I n 1995, I was hired by a large interstate law firm to handle its Florida real estate matters. No matter how hard I tried, my workload made it practically impossible for me to achieve my goal of assisting and volunteering for those less fortunate. This was my goal in going to law school. It was very frustrating. But since my compensation was based on hours worked and funds collected, I either had to leave the law and take up a new profession or become self-established, so I could control my hours worked.

While I was pondering my legal future, I received a litigation file from our largest real estate client. The good news was it involved real estate; the bad news was it was litigation. Even though my real estate caseload was increasing, my firm wanted me to handle real estate related litigation. I was a unicorn of sorts in that I was a "real estate" lawyer who could try cases and still do transactional real estate due to my experience and favorable outcomes.

The facts of this new litigation case were about something I could never make up on my own. I was about to sue a person for growing and selling roses.

Our client developed large tracts of land and subdivided them into lots for homes. Under state and federal law, the developer was required to file a set of deed restrictions and create a homeowner's association to manage the subdivision. The restrictions were designed to allow the homeowners to run the subdivision once the developer sold substantially all the lots. The deed restrictions also contained rules on maintaining each lot owner's property, including ensuring landscaping and lawns were in tip-top shape.

These types of deed restrictions have been around for years. In fact, there are still some restrictions encumbering land that require owners not to sell their lots to blacks, Jews or Catholics. Even though these restrictions are unenforceable today, the restrictions are still in the public records. I even had a transaction where a board-certified real estate attorney prepared a deed that prohibited anyone who was black, Jewish or Catholic from owning any of the lands in that transaction. Our client, the purchaser, was Jewish. I politely told that attorney to double-check his work, and the problem was solved. I even got a six-pack for pointing this mistake out to the attorney.

The lot owner, in my case, grew roses as a hobby. He had written extensively on the subject of roses and how to raise and cultivate them, including new types and colors. I would have thought his neighbors would approve of such a hobby; however, not in this case. This was because the lot owner's entire front yard was covered with roses.

The neighbors demanded our client, the developer, take immediate action in removing the roses since it still was running the homeowner's association. Letters were written to the our client by neighbors claiming the roses were a nuisance. They said people would park in the subdivision to stop and smell the roses. Cars were being parked on other lot owners' property. Our client wanted this situation resolved; he wanted the roses gone ASAP.

An old maximum says, "When the law is on your side, argue it; when the law is not on your side, argue the facts. When you don't have the law or facts on your side, pound the table hard and loud." Before researching this matter, I had a bad feeling both the law and facts were against us.

I drove up and saw the subject property. The entire front yard was covered in different colors and varieties of roses. As described, I saw people parking on the other residents' property. This rose garden had more roses than any Home Depot or Lowes.

I spent the next few days reviewing the law, reading the letters sent to our client and the deed restrictions. There just did not seem to be anything on our side to prevail in court. I was even sent a copy of the Tampa, Florida newspaper with a letter to the Editor about my client's attempt to remove the rose garden. It bashed all lawyers, including me, for bringing frivolous lawsuits and having too many commercials interfering with watching their favorite TV shows. I can't argue with someone who enjoys watching a Matlock re-run.

I was pacing in my office, trying to think of anything that might help our client's position. Then, out of nowhere, it occurred to me that I should go back to the basics and start from the beginning in my analysis of this case. Keep it simple. So, I went to my old, dogeared law school legal dictionary to see what constituted a nuisance.

After my review, I looked back at the pictures of the yard. To my surprise, I came up with an idea that might solve my dilemma and get the lot owner to settle.

What do roses require to grow? Fertilizer. How did you get fertilizer? You either go to a hardware or plant store to buy it, or you can also make your own using a compost pit. The pictures showed a compost pit up by the front of the house. We had those pits in Virginia growing up. They smelled awful and attracted insects and animals. I think I just found my legal theory to help our client have the roses removed or, at least, substantially reduced in size. I would argue the rose garden and compost pit were nuisances.

I drew up the complaint that evening. I argued the lot owner violated the deed restrictions regarding the requirement each resident have a "green and luxuriant" front yard and that the owner was creating a public nuisance in violation of the deed restrictions, including by having a compost pit in his front yard. A week after filing the complaint, I received a phone call from the Judge's legal assistant.

"Mr. Morgan, the judge would like you to appear tomorrow regarding your complaint about the roses."

"Tomorrow? Is it possible to schedule this hearing for another day? Unfortunately, my calendar is full, and I really have no time tomorrow."

"I don't think you understand. The Judge is not having a hearing. It is more of a discussion about your complaint and how he wants this situation with the lot owner handled."

At this point, my nerve endings were tingling. Under the law, you can't have a judge deal with a contested issue unless all parties to the lawsuit were invited to attend.

"Well, is the lot owner we are suing going to be there?"

"No. He has not been invited."

"Thanks for calling. I will speak with my client and get back to you about this 'meeting' the judge wants to have."

"You truly misunderstand, Mr. Morgan. The Judge is not asking you to attend this meeting. He is demanding it. Oh, and if I were you, I would consider bringing a change of underwear and a toothbrush—you may be here a while."

This had to be the first time in my life I was speechless. I thanked the judicial assistant again and immediately called our client.

I advised the client of this very unusual request. I also told the client the legal fees would definitely be more than originally discussed. The client asked for the name of the judge. Surprise, the client knew all about this judge. Years earlier, the judge went around the subdivision requesting political donations for his election as a judge. The client's prior attorneys had obtained an injunction against the judge trespassing and conducting commercial activities in the subdivision, like asking for political donations.

At this time, I was married and had a baby girl. I had a feeling if I appeared at this hearing, I might not see my daughter until after her Bat Mitzvah.

After giving this matter more thought, I advised the legal assistant I would not be attending the hearing in person but would be happy to appear telephonically instead, as we did not have zoom back then. This way, if the judge wanted me jailed, he would have to come and get me. She said she would tell the Judge about my request.

I contacted the Florida Bar Association since all attorneys and judges in Florida had to be a member of the bar to practice law. Anyone licensed to practice law, including judges, had to follow its rules. The bar was of no help. I was advised that if I was jailed, I could file a complaint against the judge. That was not an option for me. I didn't want to have to explain to my wife I had a new "jail house girlfriend."

The next day, I was advised the judge would not allow me to appear by phone for this meeting. After discussing this matter with my partner and the directors of our firm, it was agreed by all that having me attend this hearing in person was a no-win situation. I was told to wait and see what happened after my non-appearance.

A week later, I had heard nothing more from the judge or his office. However, the Gods of justice must have heard about my situation. I read that the judge was the subject of a Florida Bar ethical complaint involving the manner in which he "hinted" to attorneys appearing before him that contributions to his political action committee would be looked at favorably in any cases filed in his court.

It is said that you make your luck. I wonder if my call to the Florida Bar had anything to do with my "luck." I certainly was not complaining.

The lawsuit was transferred to another judge. The judge ruled in our client's favor, and the roses were required to be removed along with the compost pit. The client was happy about this outcome. My firm was happy, too.

After the case was decided, I notified the firm that I would be leaving. I wanted to help people. I may have won the case, but I was not happy about it. Cases like this were not the reason I became a lawyer. I decided I needed to relocate if I was giving myself a chance to see my goal through.

I was giving up a great salary and benefits. This decision to move kept me up all night. I was really nervous; however, I knew I would regret not going this route.

I decided to relocate back to Jacksonville, where I maintained a number of legal contacts. I was jumping into the deep-end pool without knowing if there was any water.

 Chapter 19

RULE ONE: DON'T TRY TO KILL YOUR CLIENT

While sitting in my office one day, I received a call from a good friend and client. She asked me to speak with her friend and neighbor.

The neighbor was hospitalized; he had cancer. The doctor told him he did not have more than 3-4 months to live. Nothing could be done other than to stretch out the death timeline. My new client was a doctor; he understood his situation. He would go home in a few days and go on Hospice.

I met my new client in his hospital room at 8 am the next morning. The client, his wife, and 2 beautiful children were all waiting for me. The look I received upon entering the room made me think they wanted to know if

I could do some sort of magic and make this whole situation go away. I could not.

After getting comfortable, we started looking into his situation both from a health diagnosis and estate planning perspective based on his assets and how he wanted his estate distributed. This took over an hour.

I put my briefcase on the floor along with my yellow legal pad. I stood up and walked over to my new client. He had tubes running from places I never knew existed. I was trying not to lose my composure. I was in that hospital room to provide the best legal advice and not to become another person who looked the client in the eyes and displayed sadness for his situation.

I asked the wife and children to leave me alone with their husband and father. I needed to be assured that the client would be legally competent to sign any documents. I did not want to embarrass the client should he have difficulty passing a standard legal competency test.

After we were alone, I began talking to the client about the news of the day; we even spoke about his religious beliefs and to see how he wanted those incorporated into his estate planning. He knew he would not be around for his children during the joyful times of their lives. Discussions and competency tests taught in law school do not prepare you for what my client was going through.

After asking my competency questions, I took off my lawyer hat. I asked him why he became a doctor and how he came to live in Jacksonville, Florida. We were just having a conversation between two individuals who went from a straight business relationship to one of friendship in the last few hours.

When I noticed he was getting tired, I retrieved his wife and children back into the room. I told them I would use the rest of the day and a good part of the evening preparing the necessary paperwork. I was already physically and mentally exhausted.

All that remaining day to about 3 AM the following morning, I was drafting, typing, and researching the law to get what he needed to be done. He wanted his wife and kids protected; damn anything else.

I went home when I was done. Shaved, showered and put on a clean shirt. I sat outside and watched the sunrise. I started thinking, what if I was in my client's situation? Could I have handled myself with the grace he demonstrated during our meeting the following day? How many more sunrises and sunsets were I to see? Who knew? What would happen to my family? Who would oversee them and provide advice when needed? You always hear people say you can't know the future, but in this case, we did.

On my drive to see my client at the hospital, I noticed one of our local liquor stores was open. I went in and bought a bottle of the most expensive bourbon I could find. I did not want to show up empty-handed, notwithstanding the large amounts of legal documents I was delivering.

The client signed all the documents. He was competent. I set a time later to go by their family home to complete the planning protocol. As I stood up, I reached into my briefcase and pulled out the bottle of bourbon from a plain brown paper bag. I asked my client if he wanted to join me in a celebratory drink. When we spoke the prior day, he mentioned that smoking and drinking were frowned upon in his religion. I did not care. It was not fair this man was going through hell and would be doing so for about the next 3 months. We are taught in law school there is an exception to every rule. Drinking at my client's bedside was one I had just invented. His wife asked if she could have some too. We all got a good laugh, passed out 3 pill cups, and I did the honors of opening and pouring the booze into the cups.

Just then, as we were each coming up with silly toasts, the client's doctor arrived for his morning rounds. As he walked into the room, he stared at his patient, me, and his wife. Then, he picked up the bottle of bourbon. He became incredulous.

"How dare you bring my patient alcohol; he's sick, he's dying, and what you are doing will only cause more harm. I am calling security to have you escorted out."

"First, nice meeting you, doctor. I don't remember seeing you yesterday, and I guess you missed those rounds."

"Are you accusing me of failing to provide my patient with the best possible care?"

"No, because I don't even know what that would consist of; however, you can continue giving your care all you want. This man is a doctor, he knows how bad it is, and we just completed in 24 hours the preparation and execution of legal documents to ensure his family's care for the rest of their lives."

"So, you think playing lawyer is helping here? Do you realize you may kill your client and my patient by your actions?"

I stared for about 30 seconds without saying a word. My office staff and family will confirm I never stay quiet that long.

"Do you believe the irony of your statement, doctor? Here is a man filled with tubes coming and going; he may die within the next 3 months, and your biggest concern is whether he could have a drink, which may kill him sooner. You need to remove your ego and yourself out the door now unless you wish to partake in our toast."

"I am leaving the room and will forget this even occurred. Good day."

We all busted out laughing. Guess what? We had more than just one cup of expensive and very smooth bourbon.

My client died about 4 months after we first met. I became friendly with his wife and kids. I was invited to one of the children's birthday parties. At this time, I knew becoming a lawyer was exactly what I needed to do with my life.

Chapter 20
THE "SLEEP" TEST

O ne of my clients had just lost her husband of over 50 years. During their marriage, the husband purchased a home in Jacksonville Beach, Florida. He loved the beach; his wife did not.

At this time, I had 3 children. Unfortunately, having a place at the beach was an extravagance, and I could not afford it. The client asked if I would be interested in purchasing it as she had no use for it. She had no children or close family.

I explained to the client that lawyers cannot go into "business" or "purchase property" for anything less than fair market value. Even in such a case, the client had to be referred to another attorney in order to ensure no undue influence was being asserted to prejudice the client.

While the client was waiting for a document to print, I looked up the beach property on the tax records website. She wanted to sell me the beach property for $150,000, the amount her husband paid for it 20 years prior.

I advised the client of my legal and ethical obligations about purchasing her beach property, especially for a below-market price. After checking with a real estate broker, I discovered the property was worth upwards of $1,000,000.

I have to admit; I was very conflicted. This investment (buying beachfront property for a 1/10th of its fair market value) would be very advantageous to our family and a heck of an investment. What to do?

I referred her to a very reputable real estate attorney to get his advice on the property's proposed sale to me.

I soon discovered the attorney referred my client to a real estate broker. The broker convinced the client she should see what offers she could get before selling to me.

I didn't hear from the client for about 6 months after this real estate deal was discussed. I found out the client sold the property to a personal injury attorney who was friendly with the real estate broker. He paid $500,000 for the property. He then razed the property, built a new structure and sold it months later for $2,000,000.

I have always been conservative whenever legal and ethical issues are involved. I worked hard to become an attorney. I didn't want my license lost due to greed. However, in this situation, I can honestly say I did not sleep well for the next few months. I followed the rules; the attorney/purchaser did not. He was walking around with $1,500,000 in his pocket. I was not poor by any means; however, I could have taken an action that would have benefited my family and still be ethical.

I had other opportunities to join or partner with my clients in other business ventures. But I just thought it wrong to put myself in a position of being an attorney and business partner of my client. I felt there was an inherent conflict of interest. That is just the way I was raised.

I still represented the client until she, too, passed. She invited my wife and me out to her club for dinner multiple times. I can say, on each subsequent visit with my client, I felt good she was able to sell the beach property for more than she thought it was worth. I protected my client as best I could. That was my duty; I started sleeping through the night again. I went to her funeral; the personal injury attorney who took advantage of her did not. I never spoke to the personal injury attorney after this episode; I felt a strong sense that he had no problem fleecing the client. I hope he was able to sleep well.

Chapter 21
MY FAVORITE FEE

Not sure if I have mentioned it, but I am a horrible businessman. I would be happy practicing and giving my advice and documents away for free if I didn't otherwise have to provide for my family and the bank holding our mortgage.

One of my "charity cases" was referred to me by a local synagogue. It was in 2010, and I was enjoying having my solo practice; I did not have anyone looking over my shoulder to determine if I was following law firm policy. It was my practice, and I set the policy and the fees.

This "charity case" involved a husband and wife who recently moved to Florida. They wanted simple estate planning. This included drafting wills and financial and health care powers of attorney. It was not a hard project.

Since my fee was pre-quoted by the synagogue, there was no discussion other than the project.

The couple returned to my office in a week to sign all the documents and complete my services. While waiting for a document to print, I inquired about the clients' background. The husband was a retired machinist from Germany, and his wife cleaned homes.

Theirs was a simple estate; however, while waiting for the documents to print, he made it known that he forgot to tell me he received a German Reparations check as he was imprisoned in a concentration camp during World War II. I looked at his arms. To my dismay, I saw the blue concentration camp tattoo on his arm. I had seen this type of tattoo on public television programs but never one right in front of my eyes.

My mother's side of the family was forced to leave Belgium before the Germans shut down the country. As a child, my mother and grandparents made it a rule that when any television shows dealt with the Holocaust, we would watch it as a family. History has a horrible way of repeating itself; my parents wanted to ensure we did not forget what the Nazis did during the war.

After the documents were signed, the clients wanted to give me a check for the work. I advised there was no charge. Getting to be their lawyer was payment enough. I wished them a good day.

On the way out of the office, the client asked if I wanted anything other than money for my work. They felt bad not paying. I told him to take the money he would use to pay me and have a great dinner with his wife.

Two weeks later, while working on a project in my office, the client returned and asked if he could have just a moment of my time. So we sat in my conference room, and he handed me a small box. I opened it and saw it was a Star of David necklace.

The client reminded me he was a machinist. He had some leftover gold from a project he was working on. So he melted the extra gold and made the necklace.

I asked how he knew I wanted that very gift. He smiled and said, "Only a nice Jewish man would do what you did for our family. I am not rich, but I can use my hands. I felt this gift you would not hesitate to take from us."

I never took that necklace off after that day. I never forgot that client and his family. But for the grace of God, had he been anything other than a machinist, he probably would not have survived the death camps. I teared up and hugged the man. That day I felt I was the luckiest man in the world. I didn't have to worry about making time to volunteer; I found an area of the law where I could work and help others. Amazing how sometimes the easiest answers are right before your eyes.

I was going to become an Elder Law attorney. Now, I just had to figure out how to make a living doing it.

 Chapter 22

WAS I AN ELDER LAW ATTORNEY AND DIDN'T KNOW IT?

Before drafting the estate planning documents for the concentration camp survivors, I was frustrated. My goal of helping others in a meaningful manner just was not happening working on real estate deals, litigation cases and drafting simple wills. It was at this time that I had an epiphany.

Practicing attorneys must accumulate a number of continuing legal education hours. I was running behind schedule with my hours. Also, I was getting bored of attending the same real estate and litigation courses just to get my required education hours.

There is no requirement for courses you take to be in your field of expertise. For example, I could take a class on how to defend DUI cases or divorce law updates. This is another anomaly in practicing law. Remember, when you graduate and pass the bar exam, you are a generalist and technically prepared to handle any case. No one leaves law school as an expert in a specific area of law.

Once, one of my firm's partners was ordered by a judge to defend a death penalty case. This lawyer's primary expertise was in dealing with securities law (i.e. stocks and bonds). How would you like it if your life depended on a lawyer who has never practiced criminal law or seen the inside of a courtroom, let alone this being his first death penalty case? The only thing this lawyer was qualified for would be helping you invest your assets after your execution.

One day, while streaming the internet for courses, I saw one that caught my eye. After reviewing the course syllabus (and noticing the class was being held on a long weekend in South Florida), I decided to attend. My eyes were wide open from the first speaker to the last. Ever see the AMC series "Better Call Saul"? There is a part in an episode where a character "finds herself." Just like me, she wanted to help people. Nothing more, nothing less. I could relate. I also never thought I would quote "Better Call Saul;" however, I love the show, and, ironically, it's about an Elder Law attorney. What are the chances?

During the happy hour after the conference, I walked up to one of the speakers, Jerome Solkoff. I saw he wrote a treatise on Elder Law and wanted his opinion on whether Elder Law would be a good fit for me based on my prior experience and goals. We spoke for the next two hours. I was mesmerized. After this discussion and a few drinks, I was convinced that Elder Law may be my calling.

Jerome told me he, too, practiced real estate and other areas of law to help pay the bills. Then, he stumbled onto a client who needed planning for nursing home benefits. He fell in love with the practice. He and I literally seemed to have the same backgrounds. If it is good enough for Jerome, then it is good enough for me. I was pumped; I think I found my calling and a way to satisfy my quest of helping others.

Elder Law really should be called Caregiver Law. Usually, when I was contacted to advise a client, it was their children making the call. The parent did not ever think their memory or day-to-day functioning was a problem. After hearing a parent repeat the same story 3 times during the same phone call, the children could figure out something might be wrong. Children have become caregivers to their parents. The children are now the parents, and the parents are the children. God must have a real sense of humor in getting back at the children for everything they did to their parents.

Elder Law attorneys, among other things, plan on how to pay for long-term care, such as nursing home care. Nursing home care can run $10,000 to $15,000 per month, depending on where the parent resides. They also prepare estate plans, help with tax-related issues, and assist in filing applications for long-term benefits. They also litigate disputed matters (i.e. when one child starts yelling at another that their mother loved him more than the other kids, etc.) such as guardian and conservatorships to see who will have authority to handle a parent's finances and health care affairs. They also assist in the probate process upon a parent's death.

Estate planning attorneys can sometimes handle these matters; however, from my experience, they do not know all the long-term planning issues and rules. In addition, tax attorneys will likely throw you out of their offices if you ever utter the term Elder law or long-term care planning.

By gosh, I would be an Elder Law attorney. Although Jerome passed away, there is really not a day gone by that I don't think about how I wished I could thank him again. By the way, his son lives in South Florida and is a heck of an Elder Law attorney. The apple did not fall far from the tree.

PART III

MY HEALTH

Chapter 23

BACK SURGERY AND 72 VIRGINS

While practicing law, I had two traumatic medical issues that materially impacted my ability to practice. The first was back surgery.

For those reading this, especially those with back issues, please take care of yourself, stretch and take time every day to have your "me" time. Don't let work hinder you from taking care of yourself. Follow my words and not my actions on this advice.

I was in an auto accident. My car was hit while sitting at a stop light. At first, I did not notice anything unusual; I just had a stiff neck and lower back stiffness. I saw my primary care doctor; he said to take some over-the-counter pain medication and call if it gets worse. It got worse.

As the person hitting me had no auto insurance, I was left dealing with my auto insurance company. I purchased coverage that I thought was sufficient. This particular policy was not expensive. However, I had to learn the hard way that you truly only get what you pay for with insurance.

My insurance company did not think the accident was bad enough to cause me escalating pain and discomfort. I could not sit and had difficulty making it through a typical work day. Basically, I was told to go on worker's compensation or go find treatment at my sole cost and expense. I took matters into my own hands.

After many second opinions, I was advised I needed spinal fusion back surgery. This presented two problems. I did not like the fact surgery was necessary, and although there were procedures short of having spinal fusion that could have helped me, they were considered "experimental" by the FDA. This meant these "better options" were not permitted to be performed in the US.

The procedure I opted for was performed in Europe; insurance would not cover this procedure. I figured out that if the less invasive surgery I wanted to pursue was performed and did not work, then fusion was all that could be done to help me. The insurance company's position was, why risk paying for two surgeries when you can pay for just one?

Even though I knew I needed back surgery, I tried putting it off as long as possible. The final straw was during my daughter's Bat Mitzvah. I could not sit; I laid down on the floor during the service and festivities afterwards. Enough was enough. I was not going to let the insurance company determine my best course of action. I am an American with a credit card; by gosh, I was going to get the best treatment I could find and worry about paying for it later.

I researched surgical options. The best one I found was performed by a clinic in Germany. The irony was the surgery was performed using an artificial disc manufactured in the United States. I was going to have disc replacement surgery in Germany using parts manufactured in the United States. You can't make this stuff up!

Upon arriving in Germany, the hospital sent a car to pick me up and transport me to the hotel utilized by the hospital. Since there was only one hotel in the town, it was not hard to figure out which hotel I was staying at.

The first thing I noticed once I got through passport control was a person holding a sign with my name on it. I try not to make rash assumptions about people. However, I could not help but notice the driver had a Mohawk, her hair was colored like a rainbow, and she had tattoos running up and down her entire body. I traveled by myself to Germany while my wife flew in the next day, something to do with needing the right clothes and extra luggage space to bring back anything she finds. I was in so much pain and on so much medicine, she could have been running illegal arms to help pay for the surgery and I would have had no idea.

I thought the driver was going to kill me, have my organs sold on eBay, and have my body dumped on the autobahn. We did not have Zoom back then. I had no idea about the hospital or its physicians other than what I read on the internet. I was in such bad shape I just did not care. I was going to Germany and trying to fix this health issue.

Luckily, my experience in Germany and my outcome were great. Although, there was just one little problem. After being transferred to my room at the end of the procedure, I was advised to get out of bed and start walking. I told the nurse I was dizzy. The nurse said that was normal.

I had my procedure performed during the time of the Iraq/Gulf war. There was heightened security everywhere, including protests for and against the war in Germany. CNN's international channel was running a loop of the same coverage and pictures of the war the entire time I was in Germany. The war on terror was on the top of my mind.

My nurse was Korean and spoke with a heavy accent. "Mr. Morgan, you get out bed immediately and tart your therapy."

"Look, I only speak English and just enough Spanish to order a beer. Did you really tell me to get up and walk? I have only been out of surgery for 2 hours. I don't think going for a walk is a very good idea."

"You are being soft. Get up! I will follow you if that makes you feel better." "Nothing would make me feel better at this moment, but I will give it the All-American try."

I got out of bed. I was shocked. After years of back pain, I had none. I almost cried. It had been so long since I did not have horrible pain.

But as the saying goes, "What goes up must come down." I fainted while in the hallway. When I awoke, the first thing I saw was a vision of a woman dressed head to toe in a hijab. She was checking my vital signs and speaking Arabic to the nurses surrounding me. My Korean nurse was running to get my doctor. Since it was Friday, I figured if this were the US, my doctor would already be on the back 9 at his favorite golf course. I was not sure what doctors in Germany do on Friday afternoons, but I was hoping it was not going to early happy hours.

I looked into this woman's eyes (very pretty blue, by the way) and said, "Did I just die? Did I go to heaven? Wait, are you one of the 72 virgins promised to me?" Sensing I might be starting an international incident, the nurses rushed me to my feet and back to bed. Eventually, my doctor appeared to check me out. Ironically, I could smell wine on his breath. I asked him what wine he likes to drink. He said anything that pours out of a bottle. I like doctors with a sense of humor (at least, I hope he was kidding).

I found out later that the woman was from Qatar. She was a doctor visiting her father-in-law, who had the same procedure as me. She heard the commotion, and her reflexes took over, and she came to my aid. I probably helped our relations with Qatar more than the last four Presidential administrations, but who cares? I'll mail my bill.

Last thing about my European medical procedure. During my appointment the day prior to the surgery, the doctor asked what I did for a living in the US. I told him I was a lawyer. He said he was glad he asked. What I did not know was that after surgery, he ordered a catheter for me. In the paperwork I completed prior to surgery, I specifically requested no catheter be inserted unless medically necessary. When I asked my nurse why I had the catheter in somewhat broken English, she said, "Doctor said you special patient and wanted to give you something to remember him by. He also say you a lawyer, and he hate lawyers."

The rest of my stay in Germany was uneventful, except for my wife's hairdryer incident at the hotel; I'll discuss that in my next book. The nurses kept me away from the other patients and their guests. Especially those from Qatar. I wonder why?

Chapter 24

THE HEADACHE THAT IS A PAIN IN THE ASS

After having my disc replacement surgery, for years, the only issue I had was some radiating leg pain. Nothing serious. The treatment was getting a series of epidurals from a pain specialist. I actually met one of my best friends, Dr. Edward Lee, who guided me through my medical journey. At least there was a silver lining to this episode. Unfortunately for me, Ed no longer does pain management.

I was scheduled for an epidural due to some pain symptoms. The epidurals lasted for a year, so they were worth it. This procedure was being performed by a doctor I had never met. He was trying to be funny while I was getting situated on the table. He was joking about all sorts of things. I assumed that he was trying to reduce my nervousness. He was not doing a good job.

When I was strapped in and ready for the procedure, I clearly remember the doctor saying he would go deep into my back to ensure the procedure worked well.

He was a regular comedian. That was the problem; he was more of a comedian than a doctor.

The procedure took only a minute. Almost immediately, I started having dizziness and a headache. My blood pressure was checked, and I was informed it was very high. Due to this, I could not leave the facility until my blood pressure was under better control.

After 2 hours, I was told I could leave. I still had a rapid heartbeat, dizziness, and a headache. I never had headaches like the ones I was having at that time. It was debilitating. I never had any of these symptoms from any other epidurals.

After not being able to sleep after the procedure, I was told to go to the ER. I received a pain shot and was sent home. This happened over 8 times in the next 3 weeks. Finally, I was admitted for further testing.

After finding nothing of any consequence from all the testing and MRI and CAT Scans, I was sent home. I was told to take pain meds, and I should start feeling better in a few weeks. I was not very confident in the diagnosis, but I figured I'd try it.

On my next appointment with my doctor, I had the same symptoms as I had immediately after my epidural procedure. I was in horrible shape, especially regarding my headaches. They were getting worse. I could not work full days; I had to lie down for hours at a time during the workday.

It was time for me to have a second opinion. I tried Mayo Clinic, Cleveland Clinic, and Cedars Sinai in Los Angeles, all of which said they dealt with headaches and bad results with epidural procedures. For 2 years, I saw a lot of doctors. All said the same thing. "Mr. Morgan, you have had all the treatment options we have available here; you are not better, and we don't see where repeating the procedures would serve any benefit."

At this point, I was desperate. The doctor and facility that performed the procedure filed for bankruptcy soon after my procedure. I had no one to go after to pay for my second opinions and any further treatments.

Then, my local headache doctor called me out of the blue and asked if I had tried a headache clinic in Chicago. When I told him I had not, he recommended I get an appointment ASAP and see if they could help. He apologized for not giving me this advice over the 2 years I was going cross country to get help for my chronic headaches. He meant well, but I still felt like strangling him after not giving me this option earlier.

I travelled to Chicago, was hospitalized and treated with a different protocol. After 2 weeks in the hospital, I felt better. Not 100%, but on a pain scale, with 10 being the worst, I was at a 2-3 level. I had hoped I could have a normal life. The headaches still bothered and hurt, but the pain was reduced significantly. Finally, I felt I could work again. I felt I had a chance to solve this problem.

Unfortunately, I ended up back at the same Chicago hospital a year later with the same symptoms as when I first became a patient. New meds and the timing of receiving meds were tweaked. It helps, but it left me in a position of not being able to work full time. By noon every day, I was at home lying down on my couch in horrible pain and discomfort

I had hoped to work into my 70's. Before the last epidural, I felt great, and the pain was manageable. As difficult as it was, I had to apply for disability with Social Security and my private disability insurance carrier. I just could not work up to the standards I expected of myself. I didn't want any client not to have the best representation because I had a headache.

I was eventually approved for disability benefits. This allowed me to pay bills by going on payment plans with my creditors. However, the biggest problem was that I was planning to put a substantial monthly amount into my retirement plan. I paid almost all of my children's college tuition. Working to at least 70 should have been sufficient to save enough for a nice retirement. But, as the saying goes, "You make plans, and God laughs." This headache condition threw a monkey wrench into my estate planning.

It's been 5 years since that infamous epidural procedure. I still have the painful and crushing headaches, and I still have to travel to Chicago to be treated, and I'm doing the best I can under the circumstances.

By the way, if you or anyone you love suffers from chronic headaches, please consider the Diamond Headache Clinic in Chicago.

Unexpectedly, my wife was diagnosed with Multiple Sclerosis. Her symptoms were triggered by heat and humidity. Coincidentally, I was just lying down on my couch all day, on disability. We both fell in love with the Pacific Northwest after taking a few trips out that way to show our kids some colleges. I figured we could both be better off in a cooler, less humid climate.

Now, we live in Spokane, Washington. We could not be happier. All of my family lives in the Atlanta metropolitan area. They all think I moved out to the Inland Pacific Northwest to get away from them. Nothing could be farther from the truth. I can still watch college football games, and the weather here is great, except for having to relearn how to drive in the snow.

I am on a local volunteer board of directors, served as a licensed ombudsman insuring nursing home patients received paper care and I'm becoming a coffee connoisseur. Although, I guess you can call me a coffee snob. Once I try all the local coffee places in Spokane, it's off to visit all the local beer breweries and wineries (not necessarily in that order).

I still perform free legal work through our local pro bono office to help those who can't afford to hire attorneys. In a weird way, I was achieving my quest of helping others. I never planned to do it under the circumstances, but I have had to endure it. The journey has really been crooked, but I am still on the road to accomplishing my goals all the same. I also have a family that has allowed me to do this. For that, there just are not enough words to express my thanks. I love you all.

🔨 Chapter 25
LAST CHAPTER?

Writing is a cathartic process for me. It makes me laugh and think about matters that should have had more significance when they happened. Of course, you can't change the past, but you surely can learn from it.

As for me, I am living in the Pacific Northwest, where I should have moved years ago. However, notwithstanding the economy and family dynamics, my sage advice is that never be afraid to do what you believe will make you happy.

I figured out at a young age that helping those less fortunate than me is what makes me happiest. Unfortunately, my physical condition prevents me from actively practicing law full time to do just that. It was becoming a lawyer that I thought would help me achieve this quest. It did, just not in the way I thought it would.

Even with my health being what it is, I still do the things that make me happy. I am a very lucky person. I only have these opportunities because of my family and their unconditional support. I only hope I am able to repay them for the opportunities they gave me.

In writing this memoir, I also discovered I married a wonderful person. She does not let her MS condition interfere with her working to help those needing rental and foreclosure assistance (she also does not use a hair dryer anymore. Really need to write a book on that one). One of our sons majored in non-profit management at the University of Oregon (Go Ducks!). He is working full-time for a charitable organization. Our daughter will fight for anyone needing a voice; she is passionate about her politics and seeing those less fortunate get any assistance they need. I could not be any prouder of them. My wife and children get their joy in helping others, too. Is it some kind of magic or brain chemistry that caused us to all be under the same roof? All I know is mine is not to question why. I am just lucky!

I am still licensed to practice law in the event my health improves. I am not sure if I will ever be able to go back to work full time, but I am following my grandfather's and father's advice to always maintain a license so I can work and be my own boss.

I still think about my uncle's advice on what law school to attend. Under the old adage, "sometimes things happen for a reason ", so goes my decision on the law school I chose to attend. I got my money's worth attending Mississippi College School of Law. I graduated with honors, aced the Florida Bar exam and had a job with a prominent law firm waiting for me at graduation. Wonder how many Ivy League law school students could say the same?

One last thing, remember that aptitude test I had to take in high school? It said I should forget college and, instead, focus on becoming a professional athlete, farmer or actor. Well, for over 10 years I served as an adjunct professor of law. When I taught my classes I had a great time doing it. I needed to keep student's attention; in doing this, I would tell jokes, really bad jokes I have to admit. But, I thought, "hey, that aptitude test said actor was a good fit for me." I wonder if I missed my true calling? No. No way. Practicing law was too much fun!

Thank you for taking the time to read my story. I will never forget the relationships I made while practicing law, and, especially, pursuing my quest to help those less fortunate. I know my grandparents are looking down and smiling.

Made in the USA
Coppell, TX
04 September 2022